EASY
JAPANESE
CROSSWORD
PUZZLES

USING KANA

RITA L. LAMPKIN

PASSPORT BOOKS

NTC/Contemporary Publishing Group

Published by Passport Books
A division of NTC/Contemporary Publishing Group, Inc.
4255 West Touhy Avenue, Lincolnwood (Chicago), Illinois 60646-1975 U.S.A.
Copyright © 1998 by NTC/Contemporary Publishing Group, Inc.
Printed in the United States of America
International Standard Book Number: 0-8442-8345-2
18   17   16   15   14   13   12   11   10   9   8   7   6   5   4   3   2   1

Contents

Introduction

Japanese/English Puzzles	**English/Japanese Puzzles**

INTRODUCTION

Of all the techniques and helps available for learning or reviewing vocabulary in a foreign language, crossword puzzles and word games are among the most effective—and the most fun. The puzzles in *Easy Japanese Crossword Puzzles* are designed to help beginning to intermediate Japanese speakers and students learn and review vocabulary, as well as to enhance both in-class and individual experience with the language.

Puzzles in this book are presented in two sections—Japanese-to-English (**waei**) and English-to-Japanese (**eiwa**). Within each section, puzzles are arranged according to difficulty and general level of language. Each puzzle is based on a particular topic related to daily activities or topics of study common to Japanese language classes, allowing you to concentrate on topics and vocabulary of interest to you, whatever your level of expertise.

All Japanese words in this book (*Using Kana* version) are given in the Japanese phonetic script (**hiragana** and **katakana**). (A *Using Roomaji* version is available for students who have not yet learned the **kana** characters.)

A complete glossary (Japanese-to-English and English-to-Japanese) is provided at the end of this book, both to allow you to cue yourself on words that are not familiar to you, and to enhance your learning experience. Following the glossary is an answer key for all puzzles.

1. いろ

	1		2							3		4		5
6						7								
				8										
9			10											
				11		12				13				
														14
15						16								
										17				
	18		19											
20				21			22		23					
			24										25	
26										27				
				28										

よこのかぎ

3. ペンキ
6. ふで
8. ぎんいろ
9. ちゃいろ
11. に、で
12. きいろ
15. しゃしん
17. いちど
19. いく
20. いろ
22. みどり
24. め (pl.)
26. しあわせの
27. おなじ
28. きょう

たてのかぎ

1. か、それとも
2. です
3. むらさきいろ
4. インク
5. しけん
6. あかちゃん
7. え
10. しろい
13. オレンジいろ
14. みます
15. えんぴつ
16. ペン
18. くろい
19. ねずみいろ
21. はい
22. きんいろ
23. やさしい
25. あかい

2. どうし

1	2			3		4			5		6		
					7								
		8						9					
10						11							
	12			13				14		15			
			16					17					
18					19	20							
			21										
22		23											
24					25		26						
	27	28	29				30						
					31								
32													

よこのかぎ

1. なく
5. うたう
7. わらう
8. かく
9. あける
10. かれ
12. だいじょうぶ
13. はなす
17. すわる
18. かえる
19. くる
23. でる
24. はたらく
25. あう
28. よむ
30. に、で
31. あるく
32. のこる

たてのかぎ

2. のる
3. およぐ
4. ねる
5. かいものをする
6. いる (いります)
8. おきる (2 words)
10. いそぐ
11. みる
14. つかう
15. たつ
16. はいる
20. つくる
21. あたえる
22. けす
24. かつ
26. とる
27. おちゃ
28. はしる
29. すべて
31. わたくしたち

3. けいようし

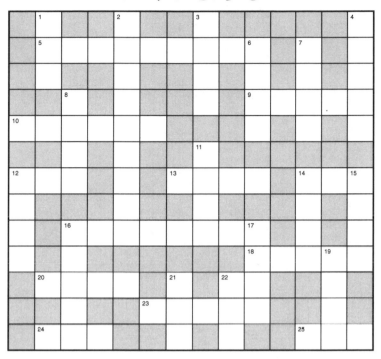

よこのかぎ

5. たかい
9. みじかい
10. きれい
12. とおい
13. ながい
14. あなた
16. りっぱな
18. はやい
20. むずかしい
22. わたくしたち
23. やすい
24. としより
25. あかい

たてのかぎ

1. あたらしい
2. うつくしい
3. かねもちの
4. しろい
6. やさしい
7. すずしい
8. ちかい
11. さむい
12. いっぱい
14. あなたの
15. みにくい
16. ちいさい
17. ふかい
19. おそい
21. かのじょ
22. でした

4. すうじ

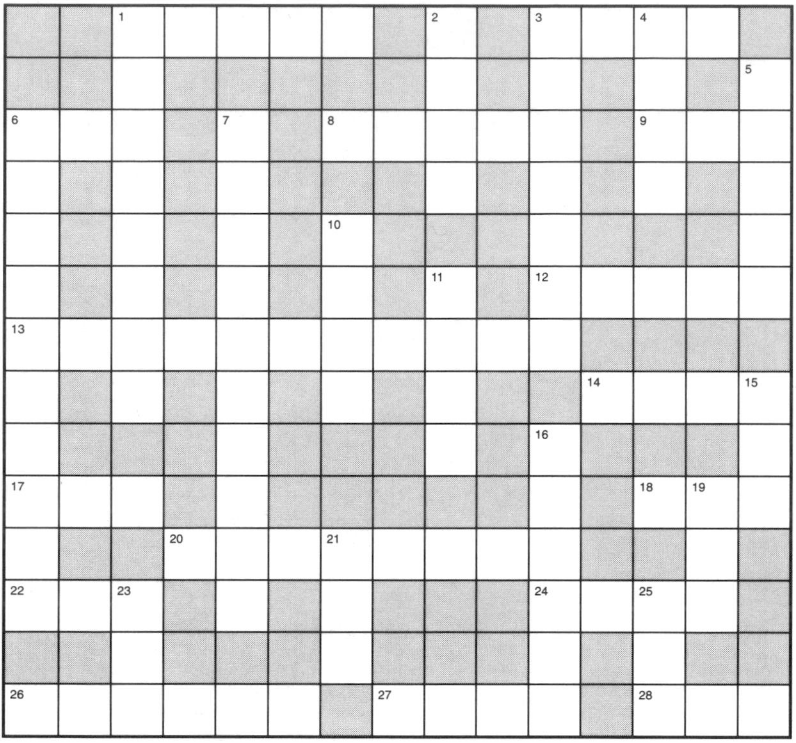

[Crossword grid]

よこのかぎ

1. さん
3. はんぶん
6. あまり
8. しち
9. に
12. はち
13. いちまん *(2 words)*
14. これ
17. びょうき
18. はこ
20. ごじゅういち
22. たべる
24. きゅう
26. きゅうじゅう
27. かれら
28. でした

たてのかぎ

1. せん
2. ご
3. ひゃく
4. おそい
5. かぞえる
6. さんじゅうご
7. すうがく
10. よん
11. たくさん
15. ろく
16. にじゅう
19. いち
21. あしのゆび
23. じゅう
25. いま

5. とき

よこのかぎ

1. きのう
4. おちゃ
6. あした
8. に
9. すべて
10. こんしゅう (2 words)
13. ひ
14. はやい
16. らいねん (2 words)
20. いま
22. おわり
23. また
26. あさ
27. いいえ
28. まつ
29. すぐ

たてのかぎ

2. ときどき
3. おそい
5. いちにちじゅう (2 words)
6. きょう
7. あめ
11. わたくしたち
12. まいにち (2 words)
13. する
15. はしりました
17. こんばん
18. よる
19. いそぐ
21. じかん、とき
24. も
25. ひる

6. カレンダー

よこのかぎ

- 1. ひる
- 8. じゅうにがつ
- 11. ひ
- 13. もくようび
- 16. くがつ
- 17. しちがつ
- 18. はい
- 20. きいろ
- 24. いちがつ
- 26. ドア
- 27. げつようび
- 28. わたくしたちの
- 29. かようび

たてのかぎ

- 2. だけ
- 3. じゅういちがつ
- 4. にがつ
- 5. かのじょの
- 6. わたくし
- 7. すいようび
- 9. はしる
- 10. じゅうがつ
- 12. どようび
- 14. しがつ
- 15. め
- 19. にちようび
- 21. おわり
- 22. みます
- 23. わたくしたち
- 24. ろくがつ
- 25. ねん
- 27. ごがつ
- 28. か、それとも

7. うちで

よこのかぎ

1. ふろば
6. くちづけ
8. ラジオ
9. ねこ
10. ドア
12. たべました
13. いえ *(pl.)*
18. テレビ
19. やね
20. きょう
23. マンション
24. にわ
27. おかね
31. わたくしたち
32. くさ
33. ステレオ

たてのかぎ

2. アパート
3. かみのけ
4. か、それとも
5. たくさん
6. だいどころ
7. っち
11. かぞく
14. さじ
15. かのじょ
16. よむ
17. まど
19. へや
21. わたくしたちの
22. おとこのこ
24. あなた
25. いぬ
26. おちゃ
28. いち
29. め
30. です

8. がっこうで

よこのかぎ

1. たぶん
6. かきます
7. クラス *(pl.)*
10. はしる
11. がくせい
15. べんきょうする
17. きょうしつ
18. すうがく
21. かのじょの
23. おわり
25. がっこう
26. いく
27. ゆめ
28. えいご

たてのかぎ

2. バス
3. ともだち *(pl.)*
4. よみます
5. きょうかしょ
8. こくご
9. うで
12. りょう
13. じゅぎょう *(pl.)*
14. め
16. せんせい
17. だいがく
19. ほん *(pl.)*
20. ぜんぶ
22. おなじ
24. いいえ
27. する

9. はんかがいで

よこのかぎ

3. かいもの
6. おそい
9. まど (pl.)
10. バス
11. いち
13. おじぎ
14. くつや (2 words)
16. に、で
17. からだ
18. ゆうびんきょく (2 words)
22. いいえ
23. か、それとも
25. わたくし
26. まち
27. としょかん
28. パンやさん
30. あご
31. め (pl.)
32. タクシー
33. まだ

たてのかぎ

1. です
2. いく
4. て
5. ひとびと
7. ひるごはん
8. ちかてつ
9. わたくしたち
12. レストラン
13. ほんや
15. あめ
18. プール
19. よん
20. かいしゃ
21. ぎんこう
24. みぎ
29. じゅう

10. いなかで

よこのかぎ

6. ふるさと *(2 words)*
9. かわ
10. かれ
11. やま
12. はち
13. はな *(pl.)*
15. おばあさん
17. どうぶつ *(pl.)*
19. です
20. おがわ
23. くちびる
25. はやし
27. メロン
29. いい
30. め *(pl.)*
31. いる *(いります)*

たてのかぎ

1. かのじょ
2. わたくしたち
3. いなか
4. おじいさん
5. き *(pl.)*
7. おかあさん
8. ちかい
10. かれの
12. はし
14. たに
15. いく
16. うで
18. わたくし
21. とき、じかん
22. ひとりで
24. いけ
26. そら
28. する

11. ひとびと

1		2					3		4				
5					6							7	
				8	9				10				
			11										
12				13				14					
													15
16		17			18				19				
					20								
	21			22									
						23		24					
25		26											
				27	28		29						
30													
		31						32					

よこのかぎ

3. おんなのひと
5. きく
7. わたくしたち
8. べんごし *(pl.)*
11. いち
12. しょくじをする
13. むすめ
16. やさしい
19. みみ
20. いちど
21. せいと
23. ひと
25. パンやさん
27. としより
29. むすこ
30. たべました
31. ひとびと
32. かわいい

たてのかぎ

1. こどもたち
2. りょうしん
3. まちがった
4. おとこのひと
6. ハンサム
7. つかう
9. おちゃ
10. め
14. せんせい
15. ともだち
17. あなた
18. いく
21. かしこい
22. せいがたかい
24. せいがひくい
26. しつれい
28. しぬ

12. たべもの

よこのかぎ

2. ごはん
5. かお
8. パン
10. のみもの *(pl.)*
11. たべもの
13. たべる
14. あご
15. ばんごはん
17. やさい
19. たくさん *(2 words)*
20. くだもの
23. すっぱい
25. じゃがいも
27. かのじょ
28. あまい

たてのかぎ

1. わたくしたち
3. ケーキ
4. こしょ
6. りょうり
7. あさごはん
9. さら
12. ひるごはん
15. おいしい
16. おみず
18. も
21. ジュース
22. たまご *(pl.)*
23. しお
24. つかいました
25. パイ
26. おちゃ

13. ひとのかお

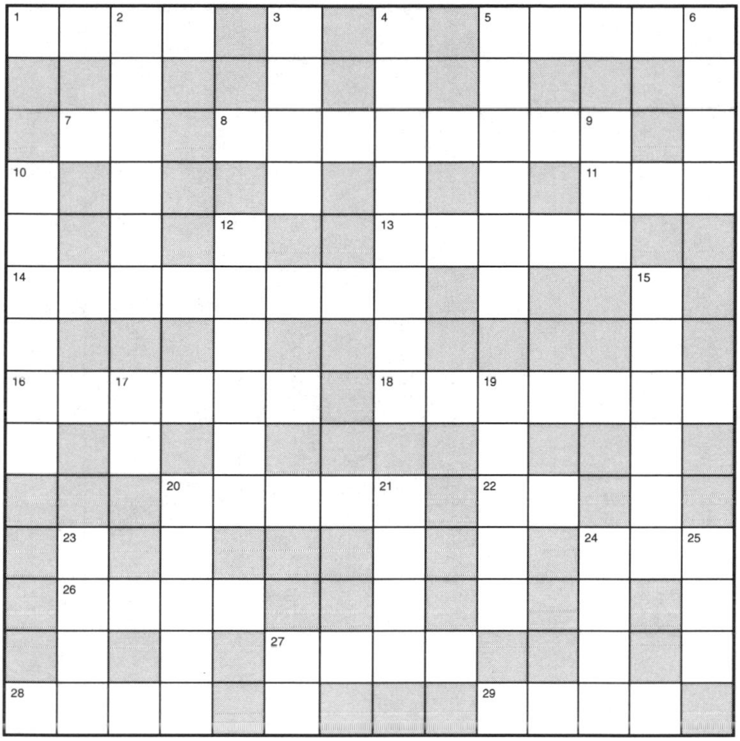

1		2		3		4		5			6

(crossword grid)

よこのかぎ

1. かお
5. は
7. かれ
8. イヤリング (pl.)
11. おわり
13. いえ
14. ひげ
16. きく
18. えくぼ (pl.)
20. はなす
22. わたくしたち
24. め
26. かみのけ
27. はな
28. いちど
29. いいます

たてのかぎ

2. ほほ
3. なみだ
4. おでこ
5. した
6. あたま
9. みる
10. にきび
12. けしょう
15. きれい
17. そう
19. くち
20. にこにこ
21. くちづけ
23. あご
24. やさしい
25. みみ
27. いいえ

14. どうぶつ

よこのかぎ

2. ぶた
4. きりん
6. とら
7. いぬ
10. むし
11. にわとり
13. みみ
16. くま
18. ライオン
20. あるきます
21. へび
22. おがわ

たてのかぎ

1. ねこ
2. ペンギン
3. うま
5. こねこ
8. ゴリラ
9. さる
12. かえる (pl.)
14. とびます
15. うし
16. とり
17. はしります
19. なまえ

15. ひとのからだ

よこのかぎ

1. かた
4. かお
7. せなか
9. げんき
11. いいえ
12. わたくしたち
14. め
15. ゆび
16. はなす
18. むね
21. くち
22. あつい
23. はな
24. て
26. しょくじをする
27. うみ
28. できます
30. かれ
31. あるく
32. うで
33. そう
34. に

たてのかぎ

2. あたま
3. うんどう
5. なく
6. ぜんぶ
8. ひざ
10. こころ
13. びょうき
14. ひじ
17. あし *(pl.)*
18. あご
19. かげ
20. に、へ
23. くび
24. かみのけ
25. します
29. いま

16. スポーツ

よこのかぎ

1. ベースボール
3. ゴルフ
6. まず
7. サッカー
10. バレーボール
11. いいえ
14. バット
15. ピンポン
16. としより
17. すべて
19. ネット
20. すいえい
23. ボール
24. テニス
25. リレー

たてのかぎ

2. バスケットボール
4. とおい
5. ボーリング
6. アメリカン・フットボール
8. できます
9. バドミントン
12. ラグビー
13. ソフトボール
18. ひくい
20. すわる
21. おとこのひと
22. いく

17. けんこう

よこのかぎ

1. ベッド
4. びょうき
6. おなか
8. はい
10. かれ
11. です
13. けんこう
15. くすり
16. あかちゃん
18. いしゃ
19. フィルム
20. に、で
21. いいます
22. わたくしたち
23. いま
25. ねつ
26. わたくしたちの
27. はしる
29. あまり
31. スポーツ
32. さむい

たてのかぎ

1. おとこのこ
2. びょういん
3. いたみ
4. ちゅうしゃ
5. くちづけ
7. あたま
9. うんどう
12. ビタミン *(pl.)*
13. ずつう
14. きく
16. からだ
17. まだ
21. ねる
22. しんぱいする
24. かんごふ
25. たべもの
28. いいえ
30. なく
31. そう

18. かいもの

よこのかぎ

1. スーパー
6. うる
11. ほんや *(pl.)*
13. デパート *(2 words)*
17. かいました
18. *(てんいんに)* きく
19. できます
21. あたらしいくるま *(2 words)*
23. ゲーム
25. いち
27. くつ *(pl.)*
29. みせ
30. に、へ
31. パンや

たてのかぎ

2. わたくしたち
3. しょうてんがい
4. かのじょの
5. ようふく
7. たべもの
8. いいえ
9. はんかがい
10. わたくし
12. すわる
14. にもつ *(pl.)*
15. そとで
16. もちかえり
20. うで
22. てんいん
24. つき
26. あいました
27. そう
28. おもちゃ

19. ようふく

よこのかぎ

1. ブラウス
5. わたくしたち
6. セーター
8. めがね
11. いいえ
15. わたくし
16. ハンカチ
17. ハンドバッグ
18. ドレス
20. きる (きます)
21. に、へ
24. あなた
26. スカーフ
27. ふくろ
30. くつした (pl.)
31. ネクタイ (pl.)
32. とけい

たてのかぎ

2. したぎ
3. みずぎ
4. ベルト
5. かつら
7. おとこのひと
9. うりました
10. せいふく
12. ジャケット
13. ジーパン
14. さいふ
17. ねだん (pl.)
19. くつ (pl.)
22. か、それとも
23. おび
25. ぼうし
28. いく
29. に、で

20. どちらへ

			1			2					3		4
	5									6			
7				8			9						
			10		11		12						
13		14								15		16	
17					18			19					
				20			21						
22		23		24									
		25				26							
	27												
		28							29				

よこのかぎ

1. いりぐち
6. したに
7. ひだり
10. にし
12. ひがし
13. ドア
15. かれの
17. となりの
19. わたくしたちの
20. おわり
22. きた
25. でぐち
26. つよい
27. とおい
28. よる
29. すわりました

たてのかぎ

1. たべる
2. に、で
3. みなみ
4. いち
5. まえ
8. ちかい
9. うしろに
11. そこ
14. みぎ
16. まっすぐ
18. に
21. まがる
22. なまえ
23. ここ
24. のる
26. むすこ

21. りょこう

よこのかぎ

2. のる *(2 words)*
4. にもつ
9. わたくしたち
11. タクシー
12. りょこうをします
13. たべました
14. こうつう
16. オートバイ
18. ふね *(pl.)*
20. きく
21. ともだち
23. すっぱい
24. でんしゃ *(pl.)*
26. じてんしゃ
27. かぎ
28. ちかてつ
29. しゅっぱつします

たてのかぎ

1. あなた
2. いく
3. たびびと
5. ひこうき
6. おりる *(2 words)*
7. でぐち *(pl.)*
8. バス
10. えき *(pl.)*
14. きっぷ
15. はい
17. うま
19. トラック *(pl.)*
20. じどうしゃ *(pl.)*
21. たのしい
22. うんてんする
25. そら

22. くにぐに

よこのかぎ

1. フランス
5. スペイン
9. わたくしたち
10. ツアー
11. みなみ
12. えいこく
14. べいこく
15. アラブ
19. みなみアフリカ
22. カナダ
23. できます
24. フィジー
25. ゆうびん
26. イタリア
28. にほん
29. インド

たてのかぎ

2. ロシア
3. いいえ
4. かんこく
6. プール
7. イラン
8. いく
10. タイランド
13. ドイツ
16. ボリビア
17. オーストラリア
18. きく
20. じゅう
21. イスラエル
22. ちゅうごく
25. おとこのひと
27. に、へ

23. しぜん

¹		²		³		⁴			⁵	
							⁶			
⁷	⁸		⁹							
		¹⁰								
¹¹					¹²					¹³
								¹⁴		
	¹⁵		¹⁶							
¹⁷										
			¹⁸		¹⁹					
	²⁰									
²¹				²²		²³				
		²⁴								

よこのかぎ

1. そう
2. しょくぶつ *(pl.)*
6. も
7. もし
9. かわ *(pl.)*
11. やま *(pl.)*
14. くるま
16. すっぱい
17. き *(pl.)*
19. しぜん
20. うみ
21. いいえ
23. そら
24. むし

たてのかぎ

1. スキーをする
3. どうぶつ *(pl.)*
4. あしのゆび
5. つかいました
6. きく
8. はな
10. に
12. おがわ
13. もり
14. くも *(pl.)*
15. はま
17. かんがえる
18. あめ
22. わたくし

24. てんき

		1		2		3		4		5			6	
7														
							8			9				
10		11												
						12		13						
14												15	16	
			17			18	19			20				
21														
					22		23							
	24		25											
26														
		27			28		29			30				
31										32				
				33										

よこのかぎ

4. ふゆ
7. つなみ *(2 words)*
8. に、で
9. あられ
10. かげ
12. あつい
14. そとで
15. です
17. あなた
18. はしる
21. おなじ
23. あらし
25. はれる *(2 words)*
26. みました
27. ふきます
29. かぜ
31. くも
32. こおり
33. と

たてのかぎ

1. さかな
2. あおぞら *(2 words)*
3. じしん
4. てんき
5. いいえ
6. あめ
9. かれ
10. ゆきがふります
11. あき
13. じゅう
16. なつ
19. わたくしたち
20. すずしい
22. なく
23. はる
24. *(あめが)* ふります
25. さむい
27. が、けれども
28. むすこ
30. しました

25. COLORS

1		2	3		4			5	
6	7								
8									9
						10			
		11							
					12				
	13								
14			15			16	17		
		18			19				
20					21				

ACROSS

2. fall
4. map
5. autumn leaves
6. to write
8. various colors
10. white
11. to bloom
12. black briefcase
13. head
14. face
16. summer
18. pencil
20. purple
21. gold color

DOWN

1. red apple
3. yellow car
4. brown shoes
5. pink
7. black
9. red light *(traffic signal)*
10. white flower
13. blue sky
15. yen
17. strong
18. station
19. moon

25

26. TIME

ACROSS

1. 1:30
5. tonight
6. endurance
8. "What time is it now?"
11. 10:30
13. age
15. 4:00
16. 9:05

DOWN

1. busy
2. "There isn't time." *(casual)*
3. "It's 3:00."
4. :04
7. 6:10
9. minutes
10. after
12. 8:00
14. 7:00
15. evening

27. AT SCHOOL (1)

	1			2		3			4	
5		6				7				
		8			9					
							10			
11	12			13		14				
	15		16							
17									18	19
		20			21					
22	23									
				24		25				
26										

ACROSS
5. Chinese characters
7. calculator
8. homework
10. dormitory
11. fool
15. goes to school
17. to write
18. not at home
20. here
21. blackboard
22. legs
24. pencil
26. teacher

DOWN
1. book
2. to walk
3. clock
4. to study
5. paper
6. dictionary
9. only
12. science
13. already
14. university
16. high school student
19. arithmetic
21. to answer
23. exam
25. next

28. NUMBERS

ACROSS
- 4. 1-2-3
- 6. 20
- 8. thousand
- 9. 64
- 12. 70
- 13. 90
- 14. 100,000
- 16. 38

DOWN
- 1. 8
- 2. 350
- 3. 9,000
- 4. 1,000
- 5. 20,000
- 7. 54
- 10. 48
- 11. 25
- 14. 10
- 15. ten thousand

29. IN THE COUNTRY

1		2		3	4		5	
6	7		8			9		10
11.								
			12					
13								14
		15		16		17	18	
19			20		21		22	
		23			24			

ACROSS

1. stream
3. bamboo
5. flower
6. went for a visit *(went to play)*
11. dish
12. neighbors
13. throat
17. watermelon
19. small town
22. carp
23. free time
24. headache

DOWN

1. grandma's house
2. spicy green sauce for sushi
4. scenery
5. woods
7. sky
8. chicken
9. studies
10. valley
14. red
15. morning sun
16. mountain
18. "Let's go." *(casual)*
20. now
21. map

30. READING MATTER

1			2			3		4		5		
6		7										
8					9			10				
				11				12				
											13	
			14			15		16				
17		18							19			
					20		21					
22	23		24				25	26		27		
28			29									

ACROSS

6. "*[I]* am reading the newspaper."
8. electric train
9. letters
10. to write
11. chest of drawers
12. next
14. age
15. as *[much as]* possible
17. to study
19. to be *(people, animals)*
22. requested *(casual)*
25. big
28. corner
29. honorific language

DOWN

1. "Did you look it up in the dictionary?"
2. book
3. "*[I]* like comics."
4. Japanese style poem
5. chair
7. sentence
9. point
10. key
11. fun
12. to make
13. to open
16. well liked
18. part, section
20. *[native]* language
21. face
23. throat
24. only
26. put down, set down
27. good

31. DOWNTOWN

ACROSS

2. shops
4. stone
5. place
7. society
9. horse
11. what?
12. subway boarding area
13. room
15. chair
16. busy
17. yellow
18. inside
19. to add
21. yes
22. tomorrow
24. furniture
25. now
26. correct
27. enters

DOWN

1. company
2. "*[I]* went to the company."
3. marketplace
5. neighboring: _____ *no*
6. "*[I]* will go out tonight."
8. one flat object
10. to wait
14. cheap
19. expensive
20. right away
21. fast; early
23. free
25. is in

32. TRAVEL

1	2		3		4		5		6	7	
									8		
9		10								11	12
13											
		14				15			16		
	17			18							
19			20			21					
		22							23	24	
25		26				27		28			
			29	30				31			
32			33								

ACROSS
1. fun
4. to walk
6. to enter
8. to wait
9. goes by subway
11. face
13. "Welcome home":
    o-____-nasai
14. mountain
15. ocean
16. noon
17. *[train]* station
18. not at all
19. yen
21. railway
22. tea
23. to listen
25. domestic *[travel]*
27. peaceful
29. to write
31. to hurry
32. cheap
33. summer vacation

DOWN
2. a transfer
3. how many?
4. red bicycle
5. drives a car
6. beach
7. sometime
9. nearby
10. Japanese meat sauce
12. to get off, get down
16. airplane
17. outing
20. far away
24. countries
25. this evening
26. long
28. meeting
29. Japanese phonetic
    characters
30. shoes

33. HEALTH

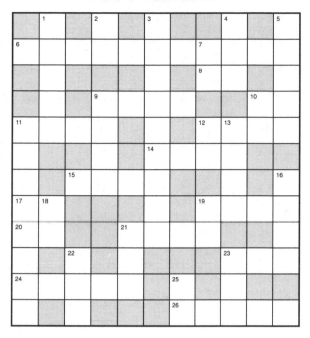

ACROSS

6. "Did *[you]* get sick?"
8. tea: *o-*____
9. a request
10. horse
11. nurse
12. "Sorry to hear it": *ki no* ____
14. to collapse
15. ugly
1/. spare time
19. dentist
20. injury
21. to tickle
23. A.D.
24. hiccup
26. injection

DOWN

1. hospital
2. cough
3. "*[My]* stomach hurts."
4. doctor
5. gets tired
7. town
9. into the bath
10. arm
11. caught a cold
12. which one?
13. excruciating
16. teacup
18. first
19. spring
21. medicine
22. belch
23. ambulance: ____*kyuusha*
25. one

34. SHOPPING

ACROSS

1. does the shopping
5. vegetables
7. fish
8. pretty
9. name
10. bow
11. 8:00 in the evening
13. every week
15. bag
17. already
18. when?
19. to write
20. shoe store
22. to reside
24. elbow
25. numerous
27. salt
29. price
31. butcher shop
32. expensive
34. now
35. rich
36. store clerk
37. chair

DOWN

1. furniture
2. take-out
3. meal
4. swell, elegant
5. cheap
6. all day long
7. honorific suffix
9. "What did [you] buy?"
10. heavy
11. clothing
12. yes
14. foodstuffs
16. penalty, punishment
21. vegetable vendor
23. chest
26. goes
28. money
30. who?
31. second floor
33. sweet potato
34. good

35. MEALTIME

ACROSS

1. "I'm hungry."
7. to stand up
8. map
9. each
10. drank *(casual)*
13. "Thank you for the feast."
15. to erase
18. many, much
19. cooking
21. pot
22. difference
24. to write
25. eggplant
26. bean curd
28. already
29. potatoes

DOWN

1. water *(honorific)*
2. to bite
3. "I will partake [of this food.]"
4. iron
5. town
6. cool
11. evening meal
12. over there
13. "Don't hesitate."
14. rice wine
16. outing
17. "Thanks."
18. to eat
20. home
23. to say
24. spicy hot
27. famous Japanese mountain

36. ANIMALS

¹	²				³			⁴		⁵

(crossword grid with numbered cells: 1, 2, 3, 4, 5, 6, 7, 8, 9, 10, 11, 12, 13, 14, 15, 16, 17, 18, 19, 20, 21, 22, 23, 24, 25, 26, 27, 28)

ACROSS

1. cries *(chirps, barks, etc.)*
3. lions
6. ten thousand
7. rabbit
8. seeds
9. okay, all right
11. turtle
12. rude
16. *"[I]* have a dog."
17. giraffe
18. sparrow
20. because
21. you
22. swell, elegant
24. dove, pigeon
25. again, also
27. "It's cute."
28. elephant

DOWN

2. fox
3. to believe
4. *"[I]* like animals."
5. goat
6. every *[day, week, year]*
8. "It's fun."
9. unacceptable, bad
10. cow
13. when?
14. "Its tail is long."
15. puppy
19. by far
23. yesterday
24. fly
25. until, up to
26. to add

37. THE CALENDAR

ACROSS

7. every [year, etc.]
9. "Today is Jan. 1"
10. age
11. 6th day of the month
13. taste
14. island
16. where?
17. summer
18. New Year's Day
19. Friday
21. fishing
22. what day of the week?
23. hospital
24. 20th day of month
27. yes
28. well or often
30. "What year is it?"
34. home
35. drawing ink
36. until when?
37. easy
38. round
39. "[I] like it."
41. 7th day of month
43. to know
44. look, watch, see
45. 1,000 years
46. again

DOWN

1. fall
2. 8th day of the month
3. Emperor Akihito's Era
4. September
5. always
6. "When is your birthday?"
7. until, up to
8. chair
10. capital of Japan
11. over there
12. Japanese phonetic characters
13. leg, foot
14. April
15. festival
16. Saturday
18. "Good morning": _____ gozaimasu.
20. "[I] am sick."
22. what?
25. "It was Tuesday."
26. book
29. mouth
30. summer vacation
31. diligent
32. "Excuse me."
33. when?
36. good
40. to do
42. throat

38. COMMON EXPRESSIONS

ACROSS

1. "I'm hungry."
5. water
7. right away
9. love
10. "Thank you for asking..."
11. "Welcome home": _____ *nasai.*
13. meeting
14. student
15. to enter
16. polite suffix
17. arm
18. "Good morning."
22. telephone
23. to hear/listen
24. Chinese characters
27. red
29. train station
30. "Excuse me for being rude."
31. one
32. "Please wait a moment": *Chotto* _____ *kudasai.*
33. from, since
34. exit
36. does
37. "It is I."
38. "Please say it": *Itte* _____
39. cat

DOWN

1. "Good night."
2. he, him
3. to do
4. house
5. "What is your name?"
6. "How are you?"
8. expensive
9. "Thanks."
10. late, slow
11. hill
12. to come
17. horse
19. "Pleased to meet you."
20. "The end"
21. "You did well."
25. "See you later."
26. "It's pretty."
27. new
28. "It's good, isn't it?"
35. yet, still

39. AT SCHOOL (2)

ACROSS

1. textbook
6. goes
8. works
10. writes on the blackboard
13. book
14. *[Thank you]* very much
16. steamship
17. "Please open it."
18. verb
20. now
21. seven
22. smart
23. student
25. is a college student
27. round
30. is present
31. early, fast
32. school
33. first day of month
34. leg, foot
36. arithmetic
37. right
38. delicious
40. pencil
41. good
42. exam

DOWN

1. nine
2. to sell
3. "*[I]* have a question"
4. again
5. hears
6. chair
7. "Excuse me."
9. studies
10. high school student
11. cloud
12. "Please write."
15. English language
19. every day
21. homework
23. "Are *[you]* a teacher?"
24. takes
26. busy
28. painful
29. to meet
31. honey
33. desk
34. blue
35. bag
39. stone

40. AT HOME

ACROSS

1. "I'm home."
3. again, also
5. family
8. only
9. "Come back soon."
10. love
12. "Please wait": _____ *kudasai.*
15. sleeps
16. chair
17. warm
18. now
19. garden
20. cold
22. "Excuse me."
23. one
24. "Welcome home.":
    _____ *nasai.*
25. March
26. music
27. guests: *o-_____*
28. to go

DOWN

1. expensive
2. "I'll be right back."
4. fun
5. household
6. "Is anybody home?":
   gomen _____
7. is laughing
10. you
11. older sister
13. happiness
14. first day of the month
19. 20,000 yen
21. sometime
23. busy
24. tea
25. cherry tree

41. PHYSICAL ACTIVITIES

					2		3		4				5

(crossword grid)

ACROSS

1. "How are you?"
4. to run
6. stood up
7. window
8. to die
9. back
12. "Are you hungry?"
14. when?
15. "My head hurts."
17. older brother
19. to be *(things)*
20. pretty, clean
21. chair
22. to write
23. moon
24. neck
25. is
27. said
28. "Please sit down."
30. to buy
34. sick
36. short:___ ga *hikui*
37. ankle
38. won't drink
40. waited
41. came

DOWN

1. interesting, amusing
2. shoulder
3. now
4. works
5. "I'm thirsty."
9. is tall
10. face
11. foot, leg
13. learns
16. didn't walk
18. pimple
19. hot
22. body
24. mouth
26. won't sit down
27. no
29. wrist
31. moves
32. plays
33. hair
35. feelings
37. tomorrow
39. mountain
40. again

42. AT WORK

1				2		3			4		5
6		7			8			9			
				10			11				
						12			13		
	14			15		16					
						17					
18			19		20						
	21						22				
23				24				25	26		
			27				28				
	29										

ACROSS

1. job
2. from 9:00 till 5:00
6. to park the car
9. stone
10. to watch
11. secretary
13. person *(suffix)*
14. "*[I]* will do it right now."
17. box lunch: o-_____
18. to write
20. to come
21. briefcase
23. clock
24. "Will *[he]* do it?"
25. horse
27. rice wine
28. store clerk
29. 1,000,000

DOWN

1. president of the company
2. sneeze
3. to go home
4. office
5. telephone
7. moves
8. to do
9. doctor
12. free time
13. employees
15. to know
16. to slip, slide
18. supervisor
19. what?
20. car
21. company
22. subway
24. test
26. ten thousand
27. honorific suffix

43. THE WEATHER

ACROSS

1. "It's raining."
5. storm
6. by far
8. typhoon
10. face
11. spring
13. always
15. hail
16. Japanese person
17. season
20. arm
21. summer
23. company
24. *[wind]* blows
25. sees
27. approximately
29. air
31. strange
33. leg
34. cloud
36. to walk
37. peaceful
38. first day of the month

DOWN

1. "It will probably clear up tomorrow."
2. usual
3. "It's fine weather."
4. cool
5. fall
7. very
9. to be *(people, animals)*
12. healthy
14. rainy season
15. warm
16. rainbow
18. tidal wave
19. Japanese bath
20. horse
22. wife
26. a little bit
28. next month
29. to cloud up
30. to hear
32. wind
33. you
35. if

44. FOREIGN FOODS

ACROSS
1. chocolate ice cream
5. soup
6. cabbage
10. fried chicken
12. bananas
13. cake
17. vanilla milk shake
18. bread
19. junk food

DOWN
1. cheese fondue
2. corned beef
3. apple pie
4. cookies
7. beefsteak
8. hamburgers
9. pineapple sandwich
11. cheesecake
14. sausage
15. gratin (potatoes *au gratin*)
16. fruit

45. FOREIGN COUNTRIES

ACROSS
1. America
3. Holland
4. Hawaii
6. Afghanistan
9. Africa
12. Indonesia
14. Iceland
15. Alabama
19. Moscow *(Moskva)*
21. Casa Blanca
22. Acapulco

DOWN
1. Ireland
2. Libya
3. Austria
5. Thailand
7. Spain
8. Russia
10. Cairo
11. France
13. Alaska
16. Pusan
17. Iran
18. Capetown: _____ *taun*
19. Monaco
20. Cusco *(Peru)*

46. THE UNITED STATES

ACROSS
1. New Mexico
3. Pennsylvania
6. Oklahoma
8. Alaska
9. Hawaii
10. Illinois
14. Grand Rapids *(MI)*
16. Minnesota
17. California
19. Denver *(CO)*
21. San Francisco *(CA)*
23. Walla Walla *(WA)*:
    Waara ____
24. Rhode Island
25. Helena *(MT)*
26. Dallas *(TX)*

DOWN
1. New Hampshire
2. Colorado
4. Arkansas
5. Wyoming
6. Oregon
7. Miami *(FL)*
8. Idaho
11. Atlanta *(GA)*
12. Missouri
13. Seattle *(WA)*
15. Oahu *(HI)*
16. Michigan
17. Kansas
18. Iowa
20. Vermont
21. Salina *(KS)*
22. Florida
24. Los *[Angeles]*

47. BORROWED WORDS

ACROSS

1. gasoline
2. bacon
3. dial
5. aspirin
7. stereo
10. jeans
12. football: *amerikan____*
14. channel
16. announcer
17. chili
18. strike
19. mousse
21. data
22. roommate
25. chimpanzee
27. ink
28. film
29. crayon
30. piano
31. personal computer

DOWN

1. garage
2. baseball
3. dozen
4. apartment
6. research
8. table
9. all right
11. questionnaire
12. full-time
13. bonus
15. recital
17. chicken
18. skim milk
20. supermarket
23. toilet
24. action
25. chalk
26. jazz
28. floor

GLOSSARY

Japanese — English

A

ago あご chin
ai あい love
aimashita あいました met
akachan あかちゃん baby
akai あかい red
akeru あける open
aki あき fall, autumn
amai あまい sweet
amari あまり too
ame あめ rain
Amerikan futtobooru アメリカンフットボール football
anata あなた you
anata no あなたの your
aozora あおぞら blue sky
apaato アパート apartment
Arabu アラブ Arabia
arare あられ hail
arashi あらし storm
arukimasu あるきます walks
aruku あるく walk
asa あさ morning
asagohan あさごはん breakfast
ashi no yubi あしのゆび toe
ashi あし leg, foot
ashita あした tomorrow
ataeru あたえる give
atama あたま head
atarashii あたらしい new
atsui あつい hot
au あう meet

B

badominton バドミントン badminton
bangohan ばんごはん dinner
bareebooru バレーボール volleyball
basu バス bus
basukettobooru バスケットボール basketball
batto バット bat
beddo ベッド bed
beesubooru ベースボール baseball
Beikoku べいこく America
bengoshi べんごし attorney
benkyoo suru べんきょうする study
beruto ベルト belt
bitamin ビタミン vitamin
booringu ボーリング bowling
booru ボール ball
booshi ぼうし hat, cap
Boribia ボリビア Bolivia
burausu ブラウス blouse
buta ぶた pig
byooin びょういん hospital
byooki びょうき sick, ill

C

chairo ちゃいろ brown
chiisai ちいさい small, little
chikai ちかい near, nearby, close
chikatetsu ちかてつ subway
Chuugoku ちゅうごく China
chuusha ちゅうしゃ injection, shot

D

daidokoro だいどころ kitchen
daigaku だいがく university, college
daijoobu だいじょうぶ all right, okay, OK
dake だけ only
deguchi でぐち exit
dekimasu できます can
densha でんしゃ [electric] train
depaato デパート department store
deru でる exit
deshita でした was
desu です is

D

doa ドア door
dochira どちら what direction?
Doitsu ドイツ Germany
doobutsu どうぶつ animal
dooshi どうし verb
doresu ドレス dress
Doyoobi どようび Saturday

E

e え picture
eigo えいご English
Eikoku えいこく England
eki えき station
ekubo えくぼ dimple
enpitsu えんぴつ pencil

F

firumu フィルム film
fude ふで brush
fukai ふかい deep
fukimasu ふきます blows
fukuro ふくろ bag
fune ふね boat
Furansu フランス France
furimasu (ame ga...) ふります (あめが) falls
furoba ふろば bathroom
furusato ふるさと home town
fuyu ふゆ winter

G

ga が but, however
gakkoo がっこう school
gakusei がくせい student
geemu ゲーム game
genki げんき healthy
Getsuyoobi げつようび Monday
giniro ぎんいろ silver, silver-colored
ginkoo ぎんこう bank
go ご five
Gogatsu ごがつ May
gohan ごはん rice
gojuu-ichi ごじゅういち fifty-one
gorira ゴリラ gorilla
gorufu ゴルフ golf

H

ha は tooth
hachi はち bee
hai はい yes
hairu はいる enter
hako はこ box
hama はま beach
hana はな nose; flower
hanasu はなす speak, talk
hanbun はんぶん half
handobaggu ハンドバッグ purse
hankachi ハンカチ handkerchief
hankagai はんかがい downtown
hansamu ハンサム handsome
hareru はれる clear up
haru はる spring
hashi はし bridge
hashirimashita はしりました ran
hashirimasu はしります runs
hashiru はしる run
hataraku はたらく work
hayai はやい early, fast
hayashi はやし forest
hebi へび snake
heya へや room
hi ひ day
hidari ひだり left
higashi ひがし east
hige ひげ mustache
hiji ひじ elbow
hikooki ひこうき airplane
hikui ひくい low
hiru ひる noon

hirugohan ひるごはん　lunch
hito ひと　person
hitobito ひとびと　people
hitori de ひとりで　alone
hiza ひざ　knee
hoho ほほ　cheeks
hon ほん　book
honya ほんや　book store
hyaku ひゃく　hundred

I

ichi いち　one
ichido いちど　once, one time
Ichigatsu いちがつ　January
ichiman いちまん　ten thousand
ichinichijuu いちにちじゅう　all day, all day long
ie いえ　house
ii いい　good
iie いいえ　no
iimasu いいます　says
ike いけ　pond
iku いく　go
ima いま　now
inaka いなか　countryside
Indo インド　India
inku インク　ink
inu いぬ　dog
ippai いっぱい　full
Iran イラン　Iran
iriguchi いりぐち　entrance
iro いろ　color
iru (irimasu) いる（います）　need
isha いしゃ　doctor
isogu いそぐ　hurry
Isuraeru イスラエル　Israel
itami いたみ　ache, pain
Itaria イタリア　Italy
Iyaringu イヤリング　earring

J

jagaimo じゃがいも　potato
jaketto ジャケット　jacket
jidoosha じどうしゃ　auto
jiipan ジーパン　jeans
jikan じかん　time
jishin じしん　earthquake
jitensha じてんしゃ　bicycle, bike
jugyoo じゅぎょう　lesson
juu じゅう　ten
Juugatsu じゅうがつ　October
Juuichigatsu じゅういちがつ　November
Juunigatsu じゅうにがつ　December
Juusu ジュース　juice

K

ka か　or
kaeru (n.) かえる　frog
kaeru (v.) かえる　return
kage かげ　shadow, shade
kagi かぎ　key
kaimashita かいました　bought
kaimono かいもの　shopping
kaimono o suru かいものをする　shop
kaisha かいしゃ　company
kakimasu かきます　writes
kaku かく　write
kaminoke かみのけ　hair
Kanada カナダ　Canada
kanemochi no かねもちの　rich
kangaeru かんがえる　think
kangofu かんごふ　nurse
Kankoku かんこく　Korea
kanojo かのじょ　she
kanojo no かのじょの　her, hers
kao かお　face
karada からだ　body
kare かれ　he
kare no かれの　his
karendaa カレンダー　calendar
karera かれら　they
kashikoi かしこい　smart
kata かた　shoulder
katsu かつ　win

katsura かつら　wig
kawa かわ　river
kawaii かわいい　cute
Kayoobi かようび　Tuesday
kaze かぜ　wind
kazoeru かぞえる　count
kazoku かぞく　family
keeki ケーキ　cake
keiyooshi けいようし　adjective
kenkoo けんこう　health
keredomo けれども　but, however
keshoo けしょう　makeup
kesu けす　erase
ki き　tree
kiiro きいろ　yellow
kiku きく　hear, listen, ask
kiniro きんいろ　gold, gold-colored
kinoo きのう　yesterday
kippu きっぷ　ticket
kirei きれい　pretty
kirin きりん　giraffe
kiru (kimasu) きる（きます）　wear
kita きた　north
kodomo-tachi こどもたち　children
koko ここ　here
kokoro こころ　heart
kokugo こくご　language
konban こんばん　tonight
koneko こねこ　kitten
konshuu こんしゅう　this week
koori こおり　ice
kootsuu こうつう　traffic
kore これ　this
kosho こしょ　pepper
kubi くび　neck
kuchi くち　mouth
kuchibiru くちびる　lip
kuchizuke くちづけ　kiss
kudamono くだもの　fruit
Kugatsu くがつ　September
kuma くま　bear
kumo くも　cloud
kuniguni くにぐに　countries
kurasu クラス　class
kuroi くろい　black
kuru くる　come
kuruma くるま　car
kusa くさ　grass
kusuri くすり　medicine
kutsu くつ　shoe
kutsushita くつした　sock
kutsuya くつや　shoe store
kyoo きょう　today
kyookasho きょうかしょ　textbook
kyooshitsu きょうしつ　classroom
kyuu きゅう　nine
kyuujuu きゅうじゅう　ninety

M

machi まち　town
machigatta まちがった　wrong
mada まだ　yet, still
mado まど　window
mae まえ　before
magaru まがる　turn
mainichi まいにち　every day
manshon マンション　condo
massugu まっすぐ　straight
mata また　again
matsu まつ　wait
mazu まず　first
me め　eye
megane めがね　glasses
meron メロン　melon
midori みどり　green
migi みぎ　right
mijikai みじかい　short
mimashita みました　saw
mimasu みます　sees, looks, watches
mimi みみ　ear
minami みなみ　south
Minami Afurika みなみアフリカ　South Africa
minikui みにくい　ugly

49

miru みる look, see, watch
mise みせ store
mizu みず water
mizugi みずぎ swimsuit
mo も also
mocha もちゃ toy
mochikaeri もちかえり takeout
Mokuyoobi もくようび Thursday
mori もり grove
moshi もし if
mune むね chest, breast
murasakiiro むらさきいろ purple
mushi むし insect
musuko むすこ son
musume むすめ daughter
muzukashii むずかしい hard

N

nagai ながい long
naku なく cry
namae なまえ name
namida なみだ tear
natsu なつ summer
nedan ねだん price
neko ねこ cat
nekutai ネクタイ necktie, tie
nen ねん year
neru ねる sleep
netsu ねつ fever
netto ネット net
nezumiiro ねずみいろ grey
ni に two
ni に in
ni, de に、で at
ni, e に、へ to
Nichiyoobi にちようび Sunday
Nigatsu にがつ February
Nihon にほん Japan
nijuu にじゅう twenty
nikibi にきび pimple
nikoniko にこにこ smile
nimotsu にもつ baggage, package
nishi にし west
niwa にわ yard, garden
niwatori にわとり chicken
nokoru のこる remain
nomimono のみもの drink
noru のる get on, ride

O

obaasan おばあさん grandma
obi おび sash
ocha おちゃ tea
odeko おでこ forehead
ogawa おがわ stream
oishii おいしい delicious, tasty
ojigi おじぎ bow
ojiisan おじいさん grandpa
okaasan おかあさん mom
okane おかね money
okiru おきる wake up, get up
o-mizu おみず water
omocha おもちゃ toy
onaji おなじ same
onaka おなか stomach
onna no hito おんなのひと woman
Oosutoraria オーストラリア Australia
ootobai オートバイ motorcycle
orenjiiro オレンジいろ orange
oriru おりる get off
osoi おそい late, slow
otoko no hito おとこのひと man
otoko no ko おとこのこ boy
owari おわり end
oyogu およぐ swim

P

pai パイ pie
pan パン bread
panya パンや bakery
panya-san パンやさん baker
pen ペン pen
pengin ペンギン penguin

penki ペンキ paint
pinpon ピンポン pingpong
puuru プール pool

R

ragubii ラグビー rugby
rainen らいねん next year
raion ライオン lion
rajio ラジオ radio
resutoran レストラン restaurant
Ribia リビア Libya
rippa na りっぱな splendid
riree リレー relay
roku ろく six
Rokugatsu ろくがつ June
Roshia ロシア Russia
ryokoo (n.) りょこう travel
ryokoo o shimasu りょこうをします travels
ryoo りょう dorm
ryoori りょうり cooking
ryooshin りょうしん parents

S

saifu さいふ wallet
saji さじ spoon
sakana さかな fish
sakkaa サッカー soccer
samui さむい cold
san さん three
sanjuugo さんじゅうご thirty-five
sara さら dish
saru さる monkey
seetaa セーター sweater
sei ga hikui せいがひくい short
sei ga takai せいがたかい tall
seifuku せいふく uniform
seito せいと student
sen せん thousand
senaka せなか back
sensei せんせい teacher
shashin しゃしん photograph
shiawase no しあわせの lucky; happy
shichi しち seven
Shichigatsu しちがつ July
Shigatsu しがつ April
shiken しけん test, exam
shimashita しました did
shimasu します does
shinpai suru しんぱいする worry
shinu しぬ die
shio しお salt
shiroi しろい white
shita (n.) した tongue
shita ni したに down
shitagi したぎ underwear
shitsurei しつれい rude
shizen しぜん nature
shokubutsu しょくぶつ plant
shokuji o suru しょくじをする dine
shootengai しょうてんがい marketplace
shuppatsu shimasu しゅっぱつします leaves, departs
sofutobooru ソフトボール softball
soko そこ there
soo そう so
sora そら sky
soretomo それとも or
soto de そとで out
subete すべて all
sugu すぐ soon
suiei すいえい swimming
Suiyoobi すいようび Wednesday
sukaafu スカーフ scarf
sukii o suru スキーをする ski
Supein スペイン Spain
supootsu スポーツ sport, sports
suppai すっぱい sour
suru する do
sutereo ステレオ stereo
suugaku すうがく arithmetic, math
suuji すうじ numbers
suupaa スーパー supermarket
suwarimashita すわりました sat

suwaru すわる sit
suzushii すずしい cool

T
tabemashita たべました ate
tabemono たべもの food
taberu たべる eat
tabibito たびびと traveler
tabun たぶん maybe
Tairando タイランド Thailand
takai たかい expensive, tall, high
takusan たくさん much, many, a lot
takushii タクシー taxi, cab
tamago たまご egg
tani たに valley
tanoshii たのしい fun
tatsu たつ stand
te て hand
tenin てんいん clerk
tenisu テニス tennis
tenki てんき weather
terebi テレビ television
to と and
tobimasu とびます flies
tokei とけい watch
toki とき time
tokidoki ときどき sometimes
tomodachi ともだち friend
tonari no となりの neighboring
tooi とおい far
tora とら tiger
torakku トラック truck
tori とり bird
toru とる take
toshiyori としより old
toshokan としょかん library
tsuaa ツアー tour
tsukaimashita つかいました used
tsukau つかう use
tsuki つき moon, month
tsukuru つくる make
tsunami つなみ tidal wave
tsuyoi つよい strong

U
uchi うち home
ude うで arm
uma うま horse
umi うみ sea, ocean
undoo うんどう exercise
unten suru うんてんする drive
urimashita うりました sold
uru うる sell
ushi うし cow
ushiro ni うしろに behind
utau うたう sing
utsukushii うつくしい beautiful

W
warau わらう laugh
watakushi わたくし me
watakushi-tachi わたくしたち we, us
watakushi-tachi no わたくしたちの our

Y
yama やま mountain
yane やね roof
yasai やさい vegetable
yasashii やさしい easy, easy-going
yasui やすい cheap
yomimasu よみます reads
yomu よむ read
yon よん four
yoofuku ようふく clothes
yoru よる evening
yubi ゆび finger
yuki ga furimasu ゆきがふります snows
yume ゆめ dream
yuubin ゆうびん mail
yuubinkyooku ゆうびんきょく post office

Z
zenbu ぜんぶ all

zutsuu ずつう headache

English — Japanese

A
A.D. きげん kigen
Acapulco アカプルコ Akapuruko
action アクション akushon
add たす tasu
Afghanistan アフガニスタン Afuganisutan
Africa アフリカ Afurika
after あと ato
again また mata
age とし toshi
air くうき kuuki
airplane ひこうき hikooki
Alabama アラバマ Arabama
Alaska アラスカ Arasuka
all day long いちにちじゅう ichinichijuu
allergy アレルギー arerugii
all right だいじょうぶ、オーライ daijoobu, oorai
all right already もういい moo ii
already もう moo
also また mata
always いつも itsumo
ambulance きゅうきゅうしゃ kyuukyuusha
America アメリカ、べいこく Amerika, Beikoku
amusing おもしろい omoshiroi
animal どうぶつ doobutsu
ankle あしくび ashikubi
announcer アナウンサー anaunsaa
answer こたえる kotaeru
apartment アパート apaato
apple りんご ringo
apple pie アップルパイ appuru pai
approximately ごろ goro
April しがつ Shigatsu
Are [you] a teacher? せんせいですか Sensei desu ka?
Are [you] hungry? おなかがすきましたか Onaka ga sukimashita ka?
arithmetic すうがく suugaku
Arkansas アーカンソー Aakansoo
arm うで ude
as much as possible できるだけ dekiru dake
ask きく kiku
aspirin アスピリン asupirin
Atlanta アトランタ Atoranta
Austria オーストリア Oosutoria
autumn あき aki
autumn leaves もみじ momiji

B
back せなか senaka
bacon ベーコン beekon
bad だめ、わるい dame, warui
bag かばん kaban
bamboo たけ take
bananas バナナ banana
baseball やきゅう、ベースボール yakyuu, beesubooru
bath おふろ ofuro
be (people, animals) いる iru
be (things) ある aru
beach はま hama
bean curd とうふ toofu
bear くま kuma
beautiful うつくしい utsukushii
because ので、から node, kara
beefsteak ビフテキ bifuteki
belch げっぷ geppu
believe しんじる shinjiru
bicycle じてんしゃ jitensha
big おおきい ookii
birthday たんじょうび tanjoobi
bite かむ kamu
black くろ、くろい kuro, kuroi
blackboard こくばん kokuban
black briefcase くろいかばん kuroi kaban
bloom さく saku
blouse ブラウス burausu
blows (wind) ふきます fukimasu

blue　あお、あおい ao, aoi
blue sky　あおぞら aozora
body　からだ karada
bonus　ボーナス boonasu
book　ほん hon
borrowed words　がいらいご gairaigo
bow　おじぎ ojigi
bowl game　ボウルゲーム bouru geemu
bowling　ボーリング booringu
box lunch　おべんとう obentoo
bread　パン pan
briefcase　かばん kaban
brown　ちゃいろ chairo
brown shoes　ちゃいろのくつ chairo no kutsu
busy　いそがしい isogashii
butcher shop　にくや nikuya
buy　かう kau
by far　ずっと zutto

C

cabbage　キャベツ kyabetsu
Cairo　カイロ Kairo
cake　ケーキ keeki
calculator　けいさんき keisanki
calendar　カレンダー karendaa
California　カリフォルニア Karifuornia
came　きました kimashita
camera　カメラ kamera
Capetown　ケープタウン Keeputaun
capital of Japan　とうきょう Tookyoo
car　くるま kuruma
carp　こい koi
Casa Blanca　カサブランカ Kasaburanka
cassette tape　カセットテープ kasetto teepu
cat　ねこ neko
caught a cold　かぜをひきました kaze o
　hikimashita
[CD] rom　ロム romu
chair　いす isu
chalk　チョーク chooku
channel　チャンネル channeru
cheap　やすい yasui
cheese　チーズ chiizu
cheesecake　チーズケーキ chiizukeeki
cherry tree　さくら sakura
chest　むね mune
chest of drawers　たんす tansu
chicken　にわとり、チキン niwatori, chikin
chili　チリ chiri
chimpanzee　チンパンジー chinpanjii
Chinese characters　かんじ kanji
chocolate　チョコレート chokoreeto
clean　きれい kirei
clock　とけい tokei
clothing　ようふく yoofuku
cloud　くも kumo
cloud up　くもる kumoru
cold　さむい samui
collapse　たおれる taoreru
college student　だいがくせい daigakusei
color　いろ、カラー iro, karaa
Colorado　コロラド Kororado
come　くる kuru
Come back soon　いっていらっしゃい Itte
　irasshai
comics　まんが manga
company　かいしゃ kaisha
cookies　クッキー kukkii
cooking　りょうり ryoori
cool　すずしい suzushii
cooler　クーラー kuuraa
corned beef　コンビーフ konbiifu
corner　かど kado
correct　ただしい tadashii
cough　せき seki
countries　くにぐに kuniguni
country　くに kuni
countryside　いなか inaka
cow　うし ushi
crayon　クレヨン kureyon
cries　なきます nakimasu
crossword puzzle　クロスワードパズル
　kurosuwaado pazuru

Cusco　クスコ Kusuko
cute　かわいい kawaii

D

Dallas　ダラス Darasu
dance　ダンス dansu
data　データ deeta
delicious　おいしい oishii
dentist　はいしゃ haisha
Denver　デンバー Denbaa
desk　つくえ tsukue
dessert　デザート dezaato
dial　ダイヤル daiyaru
dictionary　じしょ jisho
Did you get sick?　びょうきになりましたか
　Byooki ni narimashita ka?
Did you look it up in the dictionary?　じしょで
　しらべましたか Jisho de shirabemashita ka?
didn't walk　あるきませんでした arukimasen
　deshita
die　しぬ shinu
difference　ちがい chigai
diligent　ねっしん nesshin
dish　さら sara
do　する suru
doctor　いしゃ isha
does　します shimasu
does the shopping　かいものをします kaimono o
　shimasu
dog　いぬ inu
domestic [travel]　こくない kokunai
Don't hesitate　ごえんりょなく
　Go-enryo naku
dorm　ドーム doomu
dormitory　りょう ryoo
dove　はと hato
downtown　はんかがい hankagai
dozen　ダース daasu
drank　のみました、のんだ nomimashita, nonda
drawing ink　すみ sumi
drive　うんてんする unten suru
drives a car　くるまをうんてんします kuruma o
　unten shimasu

E

each　ずつ zutsu
early　はやい hayai
easy-going　やさしい yasashii
eat　たべる taberu
eggplant　なす nasu
eight　はち hachi
eight o'clock　はちじ hachiji
eight o'clock in the evening　よるはちじ yoru
　hachiji
eighth day of month　ようか yooka
elbow　ひじ hiji
electric train　でんしゃ densha
elegant　すてき suteki
elephant　ぞう zoo
Emperor Akihito's era　へいせい Heisei
employee　じゅうぎょういん juugyooin
endurance　がまん gaman
English language　えいご Eigo
enter　はいる hairu
enters　はいります hairimasu
erase　けす kesu
evening　よる、ばん yoru, ban
evening meal　ゆうしょく yuushoku
every [day, etc.]　まい mai-
every day　まいにち mainichi
every week　まいしゅう maishuu
exam　しけん shiken
excruciating　くるしい kurushii
Excuse me　すみません Sumimasen
Excuse me for being rude　しつれいします
　Shitsurei shimasu
exit (n.)　でぐち deguchi
exit (v.)　でる deru
expensive　たかい takai

F

face　かお kao
fall (n.)　あき aki

family　かぞく kazoku
famous Japanese mountain　ふじ Fuji
far away　とおい tooi
fast　はやい hayai
fax　ファックス fakkusu
feelings　きもち kimochi
festival　まつり matsuri
fifty-four　ごじゅうよん gojuuyon
Fiji　フィジー Fuijii
film　フィルム fuirumu
first　まず mazu
first day of month　ついたち tsuitachi
fish　さかな sakana
fishing　つり tsuri
five after nine (9:05)　くじごふん kuji gofun
floor　フロア furoa
Florida　フロリダ Furorida
flower　はな hana
fly (n.)　はえ hae
fondue　フォンデュー fondyuu
foodstuffs　しょくひん shokuhin
fool　ばか baka
foot　あし ashi
football　［アメリカン］フットボール [Amerikan] futtobooru
foreign country　がいこく gaikoku
forty-eight　よんじゅうはち yonjuuhachi
four minutes (:04)　よんぷん yonpun
four o'clock　よじ yoji
fox　きつね kitsune
France　フランス Furansu
free　ただ tada
free time　ひま hima
Friday　きんようび Kinyoobi
fried chicken　フライドチキン furaido chikin
from　から kara
from 9:00 till 5:00　くじからこじまで kuji kara goji made
fruit　フルーツ furuutsu
full-time　フルタイム furutaimu
fun　たのしい tanoshii
furniture　かぐ kagu

G

garage　ガレージ gareeji
garden　にわ niwa
gasoline　ガソリン gasorin
gear　ギア gia
get off, get down　おりる oriru
get sick　びょうきになる byooki ni naru
gets tired　つかれます tsukaremasu
giraffe　きりん kirin
go　いく iku
go home　かえる kaeru
go out　でかける dekakeru
goat　やぎ yagi
goes　いきます ikimasu
goes by subway　ちかてつでいきます chikatetsu de ikimasu
goes to school　がっこうへいきます gakkoo e ikimasu
gold color　きんいろ kiniro
golf　ゴルフ gorufu
gondola　ゴンドラ gondora
good　いい ii
Good morning　おはようございます Ohayoo gozaimasu
Good night　おやすみなさい Oyasumi nasai
Grand Rapids　グランドラピッズ Gurandorapizzu
grandma　おばあさん obaasan
grandma's house　おばあさんのうち obaasan no uchi
gratin　グラタン guratan
guest　おきゃくさま、おきゃくさん okyakusama, okyakusan

H

hail　あられ arare
hair　かみのけ kaminoke
hamburger　ハンバーガー hanbaagaa
happiness　しあわせ shiawase
Hawaii　ハワイ Hawai
he　かれ kare

head　あたま atama
headache　ずつう zutsuu
health　けんこう kenkoo
healthy　げんき genki
hear　きく kiku
hears　ききます kikimasu
heavy　おもい omoi
Helena　ヘレナ Herena
here　ここ koko
hiccup　しゃっくり shakkuri
high school student　こうこうせい kookoosei
hill　おか oka
him　かれ kare
Holland　オランダ Oranda
home　うち uchi
homework　しゅくだい shukudai
honey　はちみつ hachimitsu
honorific language　けいご keigo
honorific suffix　さま、さん sama, san
horse　うま uma
hospital　びょういん byooin
hot　あつい atsui
house　いえ、うち ie, uchi
household　かてい katei
How are you?　おげんきですか Ogenki desu ka?
how many?　いくつ ikutsu
hundred thousand　じゅうまん juuman
hurry　いそぐ isogu
hurt　いたい［です］ itai [desu]

I

[I] am raising a dog　いぬをかっています Inu o katte imasu
[I] am reading the newspaper　しんぶんをよんでいます Shinbun o yonde imasu
[I] am sick　びょうきです byooki desu
[I] have a question　しつもんがあります Shitsumon ga arimasu
[I] like animals　どうぶつがすきです Doobutsu ga suki desu
[I] like comics　まんががすきです Manga ga suki desu
[I] like it　すきです Suki desu
[I] went to the company　かいしゃへいきました Kaisha e ikimashita
[i] will do it right now　いますぐします Ima sugu shimasu
[I] will go out tonight　こんばんでかけます Konban dekakemasu
I will partake [of this food]　いただきます Itadakimasu
ice cream　アイスクリーム aisukuriimu
Iceland　アイスランド Aisurando
Idaho　アイダホ Aidaho
if　もし moshi
I'll be right back　いってきます Itte kimasu
Illinois　イリノイ Irinoi
I'm home　ただいま Tadaima
I'm hungry　おなかがすいています Onaka ga suite imasu
I'm thirsty　のどがかわきました Nodo ga kawakimashita
Indonesia　インドネシア Indoneshia
injection　ちゅうしゃ chuusha
injury　きず kizu
ink　インク inku
inside　なか naka
interesting　おもしろい omoshiroi
into the bath　おふろに ofuro ni
Iowa　アイオワ Aiowa
Iran　イラン Iran
Ireland　アイルランド Airurando
iron　てつ tetsu
is　です desu
is a college student　だいがくせいです daigakusei desu
Is anybody home?　ごめんください Gomen kudasai
is in, is present　います imasu
is laughing　わらっています waratte imasu
is tall　せいがたかいです sei ga takai desu
island　しま shima
It is I　わたくしです Watakushi desu

It was Tuesday かようびでした Kayoobi deshita
It will probably clear up tomorrow あしたはれるでしょう Ashita hareru deshoo
It's 3:00 さんじです Sanji desu
It's cute かわいいです Kawaii desu
It's fine weather いいおてんきです Ii otenki desu
It's fun たのしいです Tanoshii desu
It's good, isn't it? いいですね Ii desu ne?
It's pretty きれいです Kirei desu
It's raining あめがふっています Ame ga futte imasu
It's tail is long しっぽがながい (です) Shippo ga nagai [desu]

J

January いちがつ Ichigatsu
Japanese bath おふろ ofuro
Japanese meat sauce てりやき teriyaki
Japanese person にほんじん Nihonjin
Japanese phonetic characters かな kana
Japanese style poem はいく haiku
jazz ジャズ jazu
jeans ジーパン jiipan
jinx ジンクス jinkusu
job しごと shigoto
July しちがつ shichigatsu
junk food ジャンクフード janku fuudo

K

Kansas カンザス Kanzasu
key かぎ kagi
know しる shiru
koala コアラ koara

L

laser レーザー reezaa
late おそい osoi
learns ならいます naraimasu
leg あし ashi
Let's go いこう ikoo
letter てがみ tegami
Libya リビア Ribia
like すきです suki desu
limousine リムジン rimujin
lion しし、ライオン shishi, raion
listen きく kiku
little bit すこし sukoshi
long ながい nagai
look みる miru
look up しらべる、しらべます shiraberu, shirabemasu
Los Angeles ロス、ロサンジェルス Rosu, Rosanjerusu
love あい、ラブ ai, rabu

M

make つくる tsukuru
many たくさん takusan
map ちず chizu
March さんがつ Sangatsu
marketplace しょうてんがい shootengai
meal しょくじ shokuji
medicine くすり kusuri
meet あう au
meeting かい kai
memo メモ memo
Miami マイアミ Maiami
Michigan ミシガン Mishigan
milk shake ミルクセーキ mirukuseeki
million ひゃくまん hyaku man
Minnesota ミネソタ Minesota
mint ミント minto
minutes ふん fun
Missouri ミズーリ Mizuuri
Monaco モナコ Monako
money おかね okane
moon つき tsuki
morning sun あさひ asahi
Moscow モスクワ Mosukuwa
mountain やま yama
mousse ムース muusu
mouth くち kuchi
moves うごきます ugokimasu

much たくさん takusan
music おんがく ongaku
My head hurts あたまがいたいです Atama ga itai desu
My stomach hurts おなかがいたいです Onaka ga itai desu

N

name なまえ namae
native language こくご kokugo
nearby ちかい chikai
neck くび kubi
neighbor となりびと tonaribito
neighboring となりの tonari no
new あたらしい atarashii
New Hampshire ニューハンプシャー Nyuuhanpushaa
New Mexico ニューメキシコ Nyuumekishiko
New Year's Day おしょうがつ o-shoogatsu
newspaper しんぶん shinbun
next つぎ tsugi
next month らいげつ raigetsu
nine く、きゅう ku, kyuu
nine thousand きゅうせん kyuusen
nine to five くじからごじまで kuji kara goji made
ninety きゅうじゅう kyuujuu
no いいえ iie
noon ひる hiru
not at all ぜんぜん zenzen
not at home るす rusu
now いま ima
number すうじ suuji
numerous おおい ooi
nurse かんごふ kangofu

O

Oahu オアフ Oafu
ocean うみ umi
office じむしょ jimusho
okay だいじょうぶ daijoobu
Oklahoma オクラホマ Okurahoma
older brother おにいさん、あに oniisan, ani
older sister おねえさん、あね oneesan, ane
one いち、ワン ichi, wan
one flat object いちまい ichimai
one-thirty (1:30) いちじはん ichijihan
one thousand いっせん issen
one-two-three いちにさん ichi ni san
only だけ、ただ dake, tada
open あける akeru
Oregon オレゴン Oregon
outing えんそく ensoku
over there あそこ、むこう asoko, mukoo

P

painful いたい itai
paper かみ kami
park the car ちゅうしゃする chuusha suru
part ぶぶん bubun
part-time パート paato
peaceful しずか shizuka
penalty ばつ batsu
pencil えんぴつ enpitsu
Pennsylvania ペンシルバニア Penshirubania
person (suffix) じん -jin
personal computer パーソコン paasokon
petit プチ puchi
piano ピアノ piano
pigeon はと hato
pimple にきび nikibi
pineapple パイナップル painappuru
pink ももいろ momoiro
place ところ tokoro
plays あそびます asobimasu
Please open it あけてください Akete kudasai
Please say it いってください Itte kudasai
Please sit down すわってください Suwatte kudasai
Please wait まってください Matte kudasai
Please wait a moment ちょっとまってください Chotto matte kudasai
Please write かいてください Kaite kudasai

Pleased to meet you はじめまして Hajimemashite
point てん ten
polite suffix さん、さま san, sama
pot なべ nabe
potato じゃがいも jagaimo
president of company しゃちょう shachoo
pretty きれい kirei
price ねだん nedan
punishment ばつ batsu
puppy こいぬ koinu
purple むらさき murasaki
Pusan プサン Pusan
put down おく oku

Q

questionnaire アンケート ankeeto
quilt キルト kiruto

R

rabbit うさぎ usagi
racquetball ラケットボール rakettobooru
railway てつどう tetsudoo
rainbow にじ niji
rainy season つゆ tsuyu
recital リサイタル risaitaru
record レコード rekoodo
red あか、あかい aka, akai
red apple あかいりんご akai ringo
red bicycle あかいじてんしゃ akai jitensha
red light (traffic signal) あかしんごう
  akashingoo
request (n.) おねがい onegai
request (v.) たのむ tanomu
requested (casual) たのんだ tanonda
research リサーチ risaachi
reside すむ sumu
Rhode Island ロードアイランド Roodoairando
rice wine さけ sake
rich かねもち (の) kanemochi [no]
right みぎ migi
right away すぐ sugu
roast beef ローストビーフ roosuto biifu
rom (CD) ロム romu
room へや heya
roommate ルームメート ruumumeeto
round まるい marui
rude しつれい shitsurei
run はしる hashiru
Russia ロシア Roshia

S

said いいました iimashita
Salina サライナ Saraina
salt しお shio
San Francisco サンフランシスコ
  Sanfuranshisuko
sandwich サンド、サンドイッチ sando,
  sandoitchi
Santa Claus サンタクロース Santa Kuroosu
Saturday どようび Doyoobi
sausage ソーセージ sooseeji
say いう iu
scenery けしき keshiki
school がっこう gakkoo
science かがく kagaku
score スコア sukoa
season きせつ kisetsu
Seattle シアトル Shiatoru
second floor にかい nikai
secretary ひしょ hisho
section ぶぶん bubun
see みる miru
See you later じゃまた Ja mata
seed たね tane
sees みます mimasu
sell うる uru
sentence ぶんしょう bunshoo
September くがつ Kugatsu
set down おく oku
seven しち、なな shichi, nana
seven o'clock しちじ shichiji
seventh day of month なのか nanoka

seventy しちじゅう shichijuu
shoe くつ kutsu
shoe store くつや kutsuya
shopping かいもの kaimono
shops (v.) かいものをします kaimono o shimasu
short せいがひくい、みじかい sei ga hikui,
  mijikai
shot ちゅうしゃ chuusha
shoulder かた kata
sick びょうき byooki
since から kara
six-ten (6:10) ろくじじゅっぷん rokuji-juppun
sixth day of month むいか muika
sixty-four ろくじゅうよん rokujuuyon
skim milk スキムミルク sukimu miruku
sky そら sora
skyscraper スカイスクレーパー
  sukaisukureepaa
sleep ねる neru
sleeps ねます nemasu
slip, slide すべる suberu
slow おそい osoi
small ちいさい chiisai
small town ちいさいまち chiisai machi
smart かしこい kashikoi
snack, snack shop スナック sunakku
sneeze くしゃみ kushami
society しゃかい shakai
sometime いつか itsuka
Sorry to hear it きのどくです Ki no doku desu
soup スープ suupu
Spain スペイン Supein
spare time ひま hima
sparrow すずめ suzume
spicy hot からい karai
spicy green sauce for sushi わさび wasabi
spring はる haru
stand up たつ tatsu
station えき eki
steamship きせん kisen
stereo ステレオ sutereo
still まだ mada
stomach おなか onaka
stone いし ishi
stood up たちました tachimashita
store clerk てんいん tenin
storm あらし arashi
strange おかしい okashii
stream おがわ ogawa
strike ストライキ sutoraiki
strong つよい tsuyoi
student せいと、がくせい seito, gakusei
studies べんきょうします、まなびます benkyoo
  shimasu, manabimasu
study べんきょうする、まなぶ benkyoo suru,
  manabu
subway ちかてつ chikatetsu
subway boarding area ちかてつのりば
  chikatetsu noriba
success サクセス sakusesu
summer なつ natsu
summer vacation なつやすみ natsuyasumi
supermarket スーパー、スーパーマーケット
  suupaa, suupaamaaketto
supervisor かんとく kantoku
sweet potato いも imo
swell すてき suteki

T

table テーブル teeburu
tail しっぽ shippo
take とる toru
takeout もちかえり mochikaeri
takes とります torimasu
taste あじ aji
tea おちゃ ocha
teacher せんせい sensei
teacup ちゃわん chawan
telephone でんわ denwa
ten じゅう juu
ten-thirty (10:30) じゅうじはん juujihan
ten thousand まん、いちまん man, ichiman
test しけん shiken

textbook きょうかしょ kyookasho
Thailand タイランド Tairando
Thank you for asking おかげさまで Okagesama de
Thank you for the feast ごちそうさまでした Gochisoosama deshita
Thanks ありがとう Arigatoo
The end おわり owari
U.S., United States アメリカがっしゅうこく Amerika Gasshuukoku
There isn't time じかんがない［です］ Jikan ga nai [desu]
thirty-eight さんじゅうはち sanjuuhachi
this evening こんや konya
thousand years せんねん sennen
thousands せん sen
three hundred fifty さんびゃくごじゅう sanbyakugojuu
three o'clock さんじ sanji
throat のど nodo
tickle くすぐる kusuguru
tidal wave つなみ tsunami
time じかん、とき jikan, toki
time-out タイムアウト taimuauto
toast トースト toosuto
today きょう kyoo
Today is Jan. 1 きょうはいちがつついたちです Kyoo wa Ichigatsu tsuitachi desu.
toilet トイレ toire
tomorrow あした ashita
tonight こんばん konban
toss トス tosu
tournament トーナメント toonamento
town まち machi
train でんしゃ、きしゃ densha (electric); kisha (steam)
train station えき eki
transfer (n.) のりかえ norikae
travel りょこう ryokoo
truck トラック torakku
Tuesday かようび Kayoobi
turtle かめ kame
twentieth day of month はつか hatsuka
twenty にじゅう nijuu
twenty-five にじゅうご nijuugo
twenty thousand にまん niman
twenty thousand yen にまんえん niman en
typhoon たいふう taifuu

U

unacceptable だめ dame
university だいがく daigaku
until, up to まで made
until when? いつまで itsu made
usual ふつう futsuu

V

valley たに tani
vanilla バニラ banira
various いろいろ iroiro
various colors いろいろないろ iroiro na iro
vegetable やさい yasai
vegetable vendor やおや yaoya
verb どうし dooshi
Vermont バーモント Baamonto
very とても totemo
very much (as in "Thank you very much") どうも doomo
voice mail ボイスメール boisumeeru

W

wait まつ matsu
waited まちました machimashita
walk あるく aruku
Walla Walla ワーラワーラ Waarawaara
warm あたたかい atatakai
watch みる miru
water みず、おみず mizu, o-mizu
watermelon すいか suika
Welcome home おかえりなさい Okaerinasai
well よく yoku
well liked だいすき daisuki
went for a visit あそびにいきました asobi ni ikimashita
what? なん、なに nan, nani
what day of the week? なんようび nanyoobi
What did you buy? なにをかいましたか Nani o kaimashita ka
What is your name? おなまえはなんですか O-namae wa nan desu ka?
what time? なんじ nanji
What time is it now? いまなんじですか Ima nanji desu ka?
what year? なんねん nannen
What year is it? なんねんですか Nannen desu ka?
when? いつ itsu
When is your birthday? おたんじょうびはいつですか O-tanjoobi wa itsu desu ka?
where? どこ doko
which one? どれ dore
white しろ、しろい shiro, shiroi
white flower しろいはな shiroi hana
who? だれ dare
wife つま tsuma
wind かぜ kaze
Will he do it? しますか Shimasu ka?
window まど mado
won't drink のみません nomimasen
won't sit down すわりません suwarimasen
woods はやし hayashi
work はたらく hataraku
works はたらきます hatarakimasu
wrist てくび tekubi
write かく kaku
writes かきます kakimasu
writes on the blackboard こくばんにかきます kokuban ni kakimasu
Wyoming ワイオミング Waioming

Y

yellow きいろ kiiro
yellow car きいろのくるま kiiro no kuruma
yen えん en
yes はい hai
yesterday きのう kinoo
yet まだ mada
you あなた anata
You did well よくできました Yoku dekimashita

1. **いろ　よこのかぎ**: *3. paint; 6. brush; 8. silver; 9. brown; 11. at; 12. yellow; 15. photograph; 17. once; 19. go; 20. color; 22. green; 24. eyes; 26. lucky; 27. same; 28. today.* **たてのかぎ**: *1. or; 2. is; 3. purple; 4. ink; 5. test; 6. baby; 7. picture; 10. white; 13. orange; 14. sees; 15. pencil; 16. pen; 18. black; 19. grey; 21. yes; 22. gold; 23. easy; 25. red.*

2. **どうし　よこのかぎ**: *1. cry; 5. sing; 7. laugh; 8. write; 9. open; 10. he; 12. OK; 13. speak; 17. sit; 18. return; 19. come; 23. exit; 24. work; 25. meet; 28. read; 30. at; 31. walk; 32. remain.* **たてのかぎ**: *2. ride; 3. swim; 4. sleep; 5. shop; 6. need; 8. wake up; 10. hurry; 11. watch; 14. use; 15. stand; 16. enter; 20. make; 21. give; 22. erase; 24. win; 26. take; 27. tea; 28. run; 29. all; 31. we.*

3. **けいようし　よこのかぎ**: *5. expensive; 9. short; 10. pretty; 12. far; 13. long; 14. you; 16. splendid; 18. early; 20. hard; 22. we; 23. cheap; 24. old; 25. red.* **たてのかぎ**: *1. new; 2. beautiful; 3. rich; 4. white; 6. easy; 7. cool; 8. near; 11. cold; 12. full; 14. your; 15. ugly; 16. small; 17. deep; 19. late; 21. she; 22. was.*

4. **すうじ　よこのかぎ**: *1. three; 3. half; 6. too; 8. seven; 9. two; 12. eight; 13. ten thousand; 14. this; 17. ill; 18. box; 20. fiftyone; 22. eat; 24. nine; 26. ninety; 27. they; 28. was.* **たてのかぎ**: *1. thousand 2. five; 3. hundred; 4. late; 5. count; 6. thirtyfive; 7. arithmetic; 10. four; 11. many; 15. six; 16. twenty; 19. one; 21. toe; 23. ten; 25. now.*

5. **とき　よこのかぎ**: *1. yesterday; 4. tea; 6. tomorrow; 8. two; 9. all; 10. this week; 13. day; 14. early; 16. next year; 20. now; 22. end; 23. again; 26. morning; 27. no; 28. wait; 29. soon.* **たての かぎ**: *2. sometimes; 3. late; 5. all day; 6. today; 7. rain; 11. we; 12. every day; 13. do; 15. ran; 17. tonight; 18. evening; 19. hurry; 21. time; 24. also; 25. noon.*

6. **カレンダー　よこのかぎ**: *1. noon; 8. December; 11. day; 13. Thursday; 16. September; 17. July; 18. yes; 20. yellow; 24. January; 26. door; 27. Monday; 28. our; 29. Tuesday.* **たてのかぎ**: *2. only; 3. November; 4. February; 5. her; 6. me; 7. Wednesday; 9. run; 10. October; 12. Saturday; 14. April; 15. eye; 19. Sunday; 21. end; 22. looks; 23. we; 24. June; 25. year; 27. May; 28. or.*

7. **うちで　よこのかぎ**: *1. bathroom; 6. kiss; 8. radio; 9. cat; 10. door; 12. ate; 13. houses; 18. television; 19. roof; 20. today; 23. condo; 24. yard; 27. money; 31. us; 32. grass; 33. stereo.* **たての かぎ**: *2. apartment; 3. hair; 4. or; 5. much; 6. kitchen; 7. home; 11. family; 14. spoon; 15. she; 16. read; 17. window; 19. room; 21. our; 22. boy; 24. you; 25. dog; 26. tea; 28. one; 29. eye; 30. is.*

8. **がっこうで　よこのかぎ**: *1. maybe; 6. writes; 7. classes; 10. run; 11. student; 15. study; 17. classroom; 18. math; 21. here; 23. and; 25. school; 26. go; 27. dream; 28. English.* **たてのかぎ**: *2. bus; 3. friends; 4. reads; 5. textbook; 8. language; 9. arm; 12. dorm; 13. lessons; 14. eye; 16. teacher; 17. college; 19. books; 20. all; 22. same; 24. no; 27. do.*

9. **はんかがいで　よこのかぎ**: *3. shopping; 6. slow; 9. windows; 10. bus; 11. one; 13. bow; 14. shoe store; 16. at; 17. body; 18. post office; no; 23. or; 25. me; 26. town; 27. library; 28. baker; 30. chin; 31. eyes; 32. taxi; 33. yet.* **たてのかぎ**: *1. is; 2. go; 4. hand; 5. people; 7. lunch; 8. subway; 9. we; 12. restaurant; 13. bookstore; 15. rain; 18. pool; 19. four; 20. company; 21. bank; 24. right; 29. ten.*

10. **いなかで　よこのかぎ**: *6. home town; 9. river; 10. he; 11. mountain; 12. bee; 13. flowers; 15. grandma; 17. animals; 19. is; 20. stream; 23. lip; 25. forest; 27. melon; 29. good; 30. eyes; 31. need.* **たてのかぎ**: *1. she; 2. we; 3. countryside; 4. grandpa; 5. trees; 7. mom; 8. near; 10. his; 12. bridge; 14. valley; 15. go; 16. arm; 18. me; 21. time; 22. alone; 24. pond; 26. sky; 28. do.*

11. **ひとびと　よこのかぎ**: *3. woman; 5. hear; 7. us; 8. attorneys; 11. one; 12. dine; 13. daughter; 16. easygoing; 19. ear; 20. once; 21. student; 23. person; 25. baker; 27. old; 29. son; 30. ate; 31. people; 32. cute.* **たてのかぎ**: *1. children; 2. parents; 3. wrong; 4. man; 6. handsome; 7. use; 9. tea; 10. eye; 14. teacher; 15. friend; 17. you; 18. go; 21. smart; 22. tall; 24. short; 26. rude; 28. die.*

12. **たべもの　よこのかぎ**: *2. rice; 5. face; 8. bread; 10. drinks; 11. food; 13. eat; 14. chin; 15. dinner; 17. vegetable; 19. a lot; 20. fruit; 23. sour; 25. potato; 27. she; 28. sweet.* **たてのかぎ**: *1. we; 3. cake; 4. pepper; 6. cooking; 7. breakfast; 9. dish; 12. lunch; 15. delicious; 16. water; 18. also; 21. juice; 22. eggs; 23. salt; 24. used; 25. pie; 26. tea.*

13. **ひとのかお　よこのかぎ**: *1. face; 5. tooth; 7. he; 8. earrings; 11. end; 13. house; 14. mustache; 16. listen; 18. dimples; 20. speak; 22. us; 24. eye; 26. hair; 27. nose; 28. once; 29. says.* **たての かぎ**: *2. cheeks; 3. tear; 4. forehead; 5. tongue; 6. head; 9. see; 10. pimple; 12. makeup; 15. pretty; 17. so; 19. mouth; 20. smile; 21. kiss; 23. chin; 24. easy; 25. ear; 27. no.*

14. **どうぶつ　よこのかぎ**: *2. pig; 4. giraffe; 6. tiger; 7. dog; 10. insect; 11. chicken; 13. ear; 16. bear; 18. lion; 20. walks; 21. snake; 22. stream.* **たてのかぎ**: *1. cat; 2. penguin; 3. horse; 5. kitten; 8. gorilla; 9. monkey; 12. frogs; 14. flies; 15. cow; 16. bird; 17. runs; 19. name.*

15. **ひとのからだ　よこのかぎ:** *1. shoulder; 4. face; 7. back; 9. healthy; 11. no; 12. us; 14. eye; 15. finger; 16. talk; 18. chest; 21. mouth; 22. hot; 23. nose; 24. hand; 26. dine; 27. sea; 28. can; 30. he; 31. walk; 32. arm; 33. so; 34. two.* **たてのかぎ:** *2. head; 3. exercise; 5. cry; 6. all; 8. knee; 10. heart; 13. sick; 14. elbow; 17. legs; 18. chin; 19. shadow; 20. to; 23. neck; 24. hair; 25. does; 29. now.*

16. **スポーツ　よこのかぎ:** *1. baseball; 3. golf; 6. first; 7. soccer; 10. volleyball; 11. no; 14. bat; 15. pingpong; 16. old; 17. all; 19. net; 20. swimming; 23. ball; 24. tennis; 25. relay.* **たてのかぎ:** *2. basketball; 4. far; 5. bowling; 6. football; 8. can; 9. badminton; 12. rugby; 13. softball; 18. low; 20. sit; 21. man; 22. go.*

17. **けんこう　よこのかぎ:** *1. bed; 4. sick; 6. stomach; 8. yes; 10. he; 11. is; 13. health; 15. medicine; 16. baby; 18. doctor; 19. film; 20. at; 21. says; 22. we; 23. now; 25. fever; 26. our; 27. run; 29. too; 31. sports; 32. cold.* **たてのかぎ:** *1. boy; 2. hospital; 3. ache; 4. shot; 5. kiss; 7. head; 9. exercise; 12. vitamins; 13. headache; 14. hear; 16. body; 17. yet; 21. sleep; 22. worry; 24. nurse; 25. food; 28. no; 30. cry; 31. so.*

18. **かいもの　よこのかぎ:** *1. supermarket; 6. sell; 11. bookstores; 13. department store; 17. bought; 18. ask; 19. can; 21. new car; 23. game; 25. one; 27. shoes; 29. store; 30. to; 31. bakery.* **たての かぎ:** *2. us; 3. marketplace; 4. her; 5. clothes; 7. food; 8. no; 9. downtown; 10. me; 12. sit; 14. packages; 15. out; 16. takeout; 20. arm; 22. clerk; 24. moon; 26. met; 27. so; 28. toy.*

19. **ようふく　よこのかぎ:** *1. blouse; 5. we; 6. sweater; 8. glasses; 11. no; 15. me; 16. handkerchief; 17. purse; 18. dress; 20. wear; 21. to; 24. you; 26. scarf; 27. bag; 30. socks; 31. ties; 32. watch.* **たてのかぎ:** *2. underwear; 3. swimsuit; 4. belt; 5. wig; 7. man; 9. sold; 10. uniform; 12. jacket; 13. jeans; 14. wallet; 17. prices; 19. shoes; 22. or; 23. sash; 25. hat; 28. go; 29. at.*

20. **どちらへ　よこのかぎ:** *1. entrance; 6. down; 7. left; 10. west; 12. east; 13. door; 15. his; 17. neighboring; 19. our; 20. end; 22. north; 25. exit; 26. strong; 27. far; 28. evening; 29. sat.* **たての かぎ:** *1. eat; 2. at; 3. south; 4. one; 5. before; 8. nearby; 9. behind; 11. there; 14. right; 16. straight; 18. in; 21. turn; 22. name; 23. here; 24. ride; 26. son.*

21. **りょこう　よこのかぎ:** *2. get on; 4. baggage; 9. us; 11. taxi; 12. travels; 13. ate; 14. traffic; 16. motorcycle; 18. boats; 20. ask; 21. friend; 23. sour; 24. trains; 26. bike; 27. key; 28. subway; 29. leaves.* **たてのかぎ:** *1. you; 2. go; 3. traveler; 5. airplane; 6. get off; 7. exits; 8. bus; 10. stations; 14. ticket; 15. yes; 17. horse; 19. trucks; 20. autos; 21. fun; 22. drive; 25. sky.*

22. **くにぐに　よこのかぎ:** *1. France; 5. Spain; 9. us; 10. tour; 11. south; 12. England; 14. America; 15. Arabia; 19. South Africa; 23. can; 24. Fiji; 25. mail; 26. Italy; 28. Japan; 29. India.* **たてのかぎ:** *2. Russia; 3. no; 4. Korea; 6. pool; 7. Iran; 8. go; 10. Thailand; 13. Germany; 16. Bolivia; 17. Australia; 18. ask; 20. ten; 21. Israel; 22. China; 25. man; 27. to*

23. **しぜん　よこのかぎ:** *1. so; 2. plants; 6. also; 7. if; 9. rivers; 11. mountains; 14. car; 16. sour; 17. trees; 19. nature; 20. ocean; 21. no; 23. sky; 24. insect.* **たてのかぎ:** *1. ski; 3. animals; 4. toe; 5. used; 6. ask; 8. flower; 10. in; 12. stream; 13. grove; 14. clouds; 15. beach; 17. think; 18. rain; 22. me.*

24. **てんき　よこのかぎ:** *4. winter; 7. tidal wave; 8. at; 9. hail; 10. shade; 12. hot; 14. out; 15. is; 17. you; 18. run; 21. same; 23. storm; 25. clear up; 26. saw; 27. blows; 29. wind; 31. cloud; 32. ice; 33. and.* **たてのかぎ:** *1. fish; 2. blue sky; 3. earthquake; 4. weather; 5. no; 6. rain; 9. he; 10. snows; 11. autumn; 13. ten; 16. summer; 19. us; 20. cool; 22. cry; 23. spring; 24. falls; 25. cold; 27. but; 28. son; 30. did.*

25. **COLORS Across:** *2. あき; 4. ちず; 5. もみじ; 6. かく; 8. いろいろないろ; 10. しろ; 11. さく; 12. くろいかばん; 13. あたま; 14. かお; 16. なつ; 18. えんぴつ; 20. むらさき; 21. きんいろ.* **Down:** *1. あかいりんご; 3. きいろのくるま; 4. ちゃいろのくつ; 5. ももいろ; 7. くろ; 9. あかしんごう; 10. しろいはな; 13. あおぞら; 15. えん; 17. つよい; 18. えき; 19. つき*

26. **TIME Across:** *1. いちじはん; 5. こんばん; 6. がまん; 8. いまなんじですか; 11. じゅうじはん; 13. とし; 15. よじ; 16. くじごふん.* **Down:** *1. いそがしい; 2. じかんがない; 3. さんじです; 4. よんぷん; 7. ろくじじゅっぷん; 9. ふん; 10. あと; 12. はちじ; 14. しちじ; 15. よる.*

27. **AT SCHOOL (1) Across:** *5. かんじ; 7. けいさんき; 8. しゅくだい; 10. りょう; 11. ばか; 15. がっこうへいきます; 17. かく; 18. るす; 20. ここ; 21. こくばん; 22. あし; 24. えんぴつ; 26. せんせい.* **Down:** *1. ほん; 2. あるく; 3. とけい; 4. べんきょうする; 5. かみ; 6. じしょ; 9. だけ; 12. かがく; 13. もう; 14. だいがく; 16. こうこうせい; 19. すうがく; 21. こたえる; 23. しけん; 25. つぎ.*

28. **NUMBERS Across:** *4. いちにさん; 6. にじゅう; 8. せん; 9. ろくじゅうよん; 12. しちじゅう; 13. きゅうじゅう; 14. じゅうまん; 16. さんじゅうはち.* **Down:** *1. はち; 2. さんびゃくごじゅう; 3. きゅうせん; 4. いっせん; 5. にまん; 7. ごじゅうし; 10. よんじゅうはち; 11. にじゅうご; 14. じゅう; 15. まん.*

29. IN THE COUNTRY Across: *1.* おがわ; *3.* たけ; *5.* はな; *6.* あそびにいきました; *11.* さら; *12.* となりびと; *13.* のど; *17.* すいか; *19.* ちいさいまち; *22.* こい; *23.* ひま; *24.* ずつう. **Down:** *1.* おばあさんのうち; *2.* わさび; *4.* けしき; *7.* そら; *8.* にわとり; *9.* まなびます; *10.* たに; *14.* あかい; *15.* あさひ; *16.* やま; *18.* いこう; *20.* いま; *21.* ちず.

30. READING MATTER Across: *6.* しんぶんをよんでいます; *8.* でんしゃ; *9.* てがみ; *10.* かく; *11.* たんす; *12.* つぎ; *14.* とし; *15.* できるだけ; *17.* まなぶ; *19.* いる; *22.* たのんだ; *25.* おおきい; *28.* かど; *29.* けいご. **Down:** *1.* じしょでしらべましたか; *2.* ほん; *3.* まんががすきです; *4.* はいく; *5.* いす; *7.* ぶんしょう; *9.* てん; *10.* かぎ; *11.* たのしい; *12.* つくる; *13.* あける; *16.* だいすき; *18.* ぶん; *20.* こくご; *21.* かお; *23.* のど; *24.* だけ; *26.* おく; *27.* いい.

31. DOWNTOWN Across: *2.* かいものをします; *4.* いし; *5.* ところ; *7.* しゃかい; *9.* うま; *11.* なん; *12.* ちかてつのりば; *13.* へや; *15.* いす; *16.* いそがしい; *17.* きいろ; *18.* なか; *19.* たす; *21.* はい; *22.* あした; *24.* かぐ; *25.* いま; *26.* ただしい; *27.* はいります. **Down:** *1.* かいしゃ; *2.* かいしゃへいきました; *3.* しょうてんがい; *5.* となり; *6.* こんばんでかけます; *8.* いちまい; *10.* まつ; *14.* やすい; *19.* たかい; *20.* すぐ; *21.* はやい; *23.* ただ; *25.* います.

32. TRAVEL Across: *1.* たのしい; *4.* あるく; *6.* はいる; *8.* まつ; *9.* ちかてつでいきます; *11.* かお; *13.* かえり; *14.* やま; *15.* うみ; *16.* ひる; *17.* えき; *18.* ぜんぜん; *19.* えん; *21.* てつどう; *22.* おちゃ; *23.* きく; *25.* こくない; *27.* しずか; *29.* やすい; *31.* いそぐ; *32.* やすい; *33.* なつやすみ. **Down:** *2.* のりかえ; *3.* いくつ; *4.* あかいじてんしゃ; *5.* くるまをうんてんします; *6.* はま; *7.* いつか; *9.* ちかい; *10.* てりやき; *12.* おりる; *16.* ひこうき; *17.* えんそく; *20.* とおい; *24.* くにぐに; *25.* こんや; *26.* ながい; *28.* かい; *29.* かな; *30.* くつ.

33. HEALTH Across: *6.* びょうきになりましたか; *8.* ちゃ; *9.* おねがい; *10.* うま; *11.* かんごふ; *12.* どくです; *14.* たおれる; *15.* みにくい; *17.* ひま; *19.* はいしゃ; *20.* きず; *21.* くすぐる; *23.* きげん; *24.* しゃっくり; *26.* ちゅうしゃ. **Down:** *1.* びょういん; *2.* せき; *3.* おなかがいたいです; *4.* いしゃ; *5.* つかれます; *7.* まち; *9.* おふろに; *10.* うで; *11.* かぜをひきました; *12.* どれ; *13.* くるしい; *16.* ちゃわん; *18.* まず; *19.* はる; *21.* くすり; *22.* げっぷ; *23.* きゅう; *25.* いち.

34. SHOPPING Across: *1.* かいものをします; *5.* やさい; *7.* さかな; *8.* きれい; *9.* なまえ; *10.* おじぎ; *11.* よるはらし; *13.* まいしゅう; *15.* かばん; *17.* もう; *18.* いつ; *19.* かく; *20.* くつや; *22.* すむ; *24.* ひじ; *25.* おおい; *27.* しお; *29.* ねだん; *31.* にくや; *32.* たかい; *34.* いま; *35.* かねもち; *36.* てんいん; *37.* いす. **Down:** *1.* かぐ; *2.* もちかえり; *3.* しょくじ; *4.* すてき; *5.* やすい; *6.* いちにちじゅう; *7.* さま; *9.* なにをかいましたか; *10.* おもい; *11.* ようふく; *12.* はい; *14.* しょくひん; *16.* ばつ; *21.* やおや; *23.* むね; *26.* いきます; *28.* おかね; *30.* だれ; *31.* にかい; *33.* いも; *34.* いい.

35. MEALTIME Across: *1.* おなかがすいています; *7.* たつ; *8.* ちず; *9.* ずつ; *10.* のんだ; *13.* ごちそうさまでした; *15.* けす; *18.* たくさん; *19.* りょうり; *21.* なべ; *22.* ちがい; *24.* かく; *25.* なす; *26.* とうふ; *28.* もう; *29.* じゃがいも. **Down:** *1.* あずき; *2.* かむ; *3.* いただきます; *4.* てつ; *5.* よち; *8.* すずしい; *11.* ゆうしょく; *12.* あそこ; *13.* ごえんりょなく; *14.* さけ; *16.* えんそく; *17.* ありがとう; *18.* たべる; *20.* うち; *23.* いう; *24.* からい; *27.* ふじ.

36. ANIMALS Across: *1.* なきます; *3.* しし; *6.* まん; *7.* うさぎ; *8.* たね; *9.* だいじょうぶ; *11.* かめ; *12.* しつれい; *16.* いぬをかっています; *17.* きりん; *18.* すずめ; *20.* ので; *21.* あなた; *22.* すてき; *24.* はと; *25.* また; *27.* かわいいです; *28.* ぞう. **Down:** *2.* きつね; *3.* しんじる; *4.* どうぶつがすきです; *5.* やぎ; *6.* まい; *8.* たのしいです; *9.* だめ; *10.* うし; *13.* いつ; *14.* しっぽがながい; *15.* こいぬ; *19.* ずっと; *23.* さのう; *24.* はえ; *25.* まで; *26.* たる.

37. CALENDAR Across: *7.* まい; *9.* きょうはいちがつついたちです; *10.* とし; *11.* むいか; *13.* あじ; *14.* しま; *16.* どこ; *17.* なつ; *18.* おしょうがつ; *19.* きんようび; *21.* つり; *22.* なんようび; *23.* びょういん; *24.* はつか; *27.* はい; *28.* よく; *30.* なんねんですか; *34.* うち; *35.* すみ; *36.* いつまで; *37.* やさしい; *38.* まるい; *39.* すきです; *41.* なのか; *43.* しる; *44.* みる; *45.* せんねん; *46.* また. **Down:** *1.* あき; *2.* ようか; *3.* へいせい; *4.* くがつ; *5.* いつも; *6.* おたんじょうびはいつですか; *7.* まで; *8.* いす; *10.* とうきょう; *11.* むこう; *12.* かな; *13.* あし; *14.* しがつ; *15.* まつり; *16.* どようび; *18.* おはよう; *20.* びょうきです; *22.* なん; *25.* かようびでした; *26.* ほん; *29.* くち; *30.* なつやすみ; *31.* ねっしん; *32.* すみません; *33.* いつ; *36.* いい; *40.* する; *42.* のど.

38. COMMON EXPRESSIONS Across: *1.* おなかがすいています; *7.* すぐ; *9.* あい; *10.* おかげさまで; *11.* おかえり; *13.* かい; *14.* がくせい; *15.* はいる; *16.* さん; *17.* うで; *18.* おはようございます; *22.* でんわ; *23.* きく; *24.* かんじ; *27.* あかい; *29.* えき; *30.* しつれいします; *31.* いち; *32.* まって; *33.* から; *34.* でぐち; *36.* します; *37.* わたくしです; *38.* ください; *39.* ねこ. **Down:** *1.* おやすみなさい; *2.* かれ; *3.* する; *4.* いえ; *5.* おなまえはなんですか; *6.* おげんきですか; *8.* たかい; *9.* ありがとう; *10.* おそい; *11.* おか; *12.* くる; *17.* うま; *19.* はじめまして; *20.* おわり; *21.* よくできました; *25.* じゃまた; *26.* きれいです; *27.* あたらしい; *28.* いいですね; *35.* まだ.

39. AT SCHOOL (2) Across: *1.* きょうかしょ; *6.* いきます; *8.* はたらきます; *10.* こくばんにかきます; *13.* ほん; *14.* どうも; *16.* きせん; *17.* あけてください; *18.* どうし; *20.* いま; *21.* しち; *22.* かしこい; *23.* せいと; *25.* だいがくせいです; *27.* まるい; *30.* います; *31.* はやい; *32.* がっこう; *33.* ついたち; *34.* あし; *36.* すうがく; *37.* みぎ; *38.* おいしい; *40.* えんぴつ; *41.* いい; *42.* しけん. **Down:** *1.* きゅう; *2.* うる; *3.* しつもんがあります; *4.* また; *5.* ききます; *6.* いす; *7.* すみません; *9.* べんきょうします; *10.* こうこうせい; *11.* くも; *12.* かいてください; *15.* えいご; *19.* まいにち; *21.*

しゅくだい; 23. せんせいですか; 24. とります; 26. いそがしい; 28. いたい; 29. あう; 31. はちみ
つ; 33. つくえ; 34. あおい; 35. かばん; 39. いし.

40. AT HOME Across: 1. ただいま; 3. また; 5. かぞく; 8. だけ; 9. いっていらっしゃい; 10. あい;
12. まって; 15. ねます; 16. いす; 17. あたたかい; 18. いま; 19. にわ; 20. さむい; 22. すみません;
23. いち; 24. おかえり; 25. さんがつ; 26. おんがく; 27. きゃくさま; 28. いく. **Down:** 1. たかい;
2. いってきます; 4. たのしい; 5. かてい; 6. ください; 7. わらっています; 10. あなた; 11. おねえさ
ん; 13. しあわせ; 14. ついたち; 19. にまんえん; 21. いつか; 23. いそがしい; 24. おちゃ; 25. さく
ら.

41. PHYSICAL ACTIVITIES Across: 1. おげんきですか; 4. はしる; 6. たちました; 7. まど; 8. しぬ;
9. せなか; 12. おなかがすきましたか; 14. いつ; 15. あたまがいたいです; 17. あに; 19. ある; 20.
きれい; 21. いす; 22. かく; 23. つき; 24. くび; 25. です; 27. いいました; 28. すわってください;
30. かう; 34. びょうき; 36. せい; 37. あしくび; 38. のみません; 40. まちました; 41. きました.
Down: 1. おもしろい; 2. かた; 3. いま; 4. はたらきます; 5. のどがかわきました; 9. せいがたかい
です; 10. かお; 11. あし; 13. ならいます; 16. あるきませんでした; 18. にきび; 19. あつい; 22. か
らだ; 24. くち; 26. すわります; 27. いいえ; 29. てくび; 31. うごきます; 32. あそびます; 33. か
みのけ; 35. きもち; 37. あした; 39. やま; 40. また.

42. AT WORK Across: 1. しごと 2. くじからごじまで; 6. ちゅうしゃする; 9. いし; 10. みる; 11. ひ
しょ; 13. じん; 14. いますぐします; 17. べんとう; 18. かく; 20. くる; 21. かばん; 23. とけい; 24.
しますか; 25. うま; 27. さけ; 28. てんいん; 29. ひゃくまん. **Down:** 1. しゃちょう; 2. くしゃみ;
3. かえる; 4. じむしょ; 5. でんわ; 7. うごきます; 8. する; 9. いしゃ; 12. ひま; 13. じゅうぎょうい
ん; 15. しる; 16. すべる; 18. かんとく; 19. なん; 20. くるま; 21. かいしゃ; 22. ちかてつ; 24. しけ
ん; 26. まん; 27. さま.

43. THE WEATHER Across: 1. あめがふっています; 5. あらし; 6. ずっと; 8. たいふう; 10. かお;
11. はる; 13. いつも; 15. あられ; 16. にほんじん; 17. きせつ; 20. うで; 21. なつ; 23. かいしゃ;
24. ふきます; 25. みます; 27. ごろ; 29. くうき; 31. おかしい; 33. あし; 34. くも; 36. あるく; 37.
しずか; 38. ついたち. **Down:** 1. あしたはれるでしょう; 2. ふつう; 3. いいおてんきです; 4. すず
しい; 5. あき; 7. とても; 9. いる; 12. げんき; 14. つゆ; 15. あたたかい; 16. にじ; 18. つなみ; 19.
おふろ; 20. うま; 22. つま; 26. すこし; 28. らいげつ; 29. くもる; 30. きく; 32. かぜ; 33. あなた;
35. もし.

44. FOREIGN FOODS Across: 1. チョコレートアイスクリーム; 5. スープ; 6. キャベツ; 10. フライ
ドチキン; 12. バナナ; 13. ケーキ; 17. バニラミルクセーキ; 18. パン; 19. ジャンクフード. **Down:**
1. チーズフォンデュ; 2. コンビーフ; 3. アップルパイ; 4. クッキー; 7. ビフテキ; 8. ハンバーガ
ー; 9. パイナップルサンド; 11. チーズケーキ; 14. ソーセージ; 15. グラタン; 16. フルーツ.

45. FOREIGN COUNTRIES Across: 1. アメリカ; 3. オランダ; 4. ハワイ; 6. アフガニスタン; 9. ア
フリカ; 12. インドネシア; 14. アイスランド; 15. アラバマ; 19. モスクワ; 21. カサブランカ; 22.
アカプルコ. **Down:** 1. アイルランド; 2. リビア; 3. オーストリア; 5. タイランド; 7. スペイン; 8.
ロシア; 10. カイロ; 11. フランス; 13. アラスカ; 16. プサン; 17. イラン; 18. ケープ; 19. モナコ;
20. クスコ.

46. THE UNITED STATES Across: 1. ニューメキシコ; 3. ペンシルバニア; 6. オクラホマ; 8. アラス
カ; 9. ハワイ; 10. イリノイ; 14. グランドラピッズ; 16. ミネソタ; 17. カリフォルニア; 19. デンバ
ー; 21. サンフランシスコ; 23. ワーラ; 24. ロードアイランド; 25. ヘレナ; 26. ダラス. **Down:** 1.
ニューハンプシャー; 2. コロラド; 4. アーカンソー; 5. ワイオミング; 6. オレゴン; 7. マイアミ; 8.
アイダホ; 11. アトランタ; 12. ミズーリ; 13. シアトル; 15. オアフ; 16. ミシガン; 17. カンザス; 18.
アイオワ; 20. バーモント; 21. サライナ; 22. フロリダ 24. ロス.

47. BORROWED WORDS Across: 1. ガソリン; 2. ベーコン; 3. ダイヤル; 5. アスピリン; 7. ステレ
オ; 10. ジーパン; 12. フットボール; 14. チャンネル; 16. アナウンサー; 17. チリ; 18. ストライキ;
19. ムース; 21. データ; 22. ルームメート; 25. チンパンジー; 27. インク; 28. フィルム; 29. クレ
ヨン; 30. ピアノ; 31. パーソコン. **Down:** 1. ガレージ; 2. ベースボール; 3. ダース; 4. アパート;
6. リサーチ; 8. テーブル; 9. オーライ; 11. アンケート; 12. フルタイム; 13. ボーナス; 15. リサイ
タル; 17. チキン; 18. スキムミルク; 20. スーパー; 23. トイレ; 24. アクション; 25. チョーク; 26.
ジャズ; 28. フロア.